Black Odyssey

THE CASE OF THE

SLAVE SHIP *AMISTAD*

MARY CABLE

PENGUIN BOOKS

PENGUIN BOOKS
Published by the Penguin Group
Penguin Group (USA) Inc., 375 Hudson Street, New York, New York 10014, U.S.A.
Penguin Books Ltd, 80 Strand, London WC2R 0RL, England
Penguin Books Australia Ltd, 250 Camberwell Road, Camberwell, Victoria 3124, Australia
Penguin Books Canada Ltd, 10 Alcorn Avenue, Toronto, Ontario, Canada M4V 3B2
Penguin Books India (P) Ltd, 11 Community Centre, Panchsheel Park, New Delhi – 110 017, India
Penguin Books (N.Z.) Ltd, Cnr Rosedale and Airborne Roads, Albany, Auckland, New Zealand
Penguin Books (South Africa) (Pty) Ltd, 24 Sturdee Avenue,
Rosebank, Johannesburg 2196, South Africa

Penguin Books Ltd, Registered Offices: 80 Strand, London WC2R 0RL, England

First published in the United States of America by
The Viking Press, Inc. 1971
Published in Penguin Books 1977

1 3 5 7 9 10 8 6 4 2

Copyright © Mary Cable, 1971
All rights reserved

ACKNOWLEDGMENT

Massachusetts Historical Society: Quotations from the Adams Papers are from
the microfilm edition, by permission of the Massachusetts Historical Society.

LIBRARY OF CONGRESS CATALOGING IN PUBLICATION DATA
Cable, Mary.
Black odyssey.
Bibliography: p.
Includes index.
ISBN 0 14 20.0424 3
1. Amistad (Schooner).   2. Slavery in the United States—Insurrections, etc.
I. Title.
[E447.C24   1997]   382'.44   77-22007

Printed in the United States of America
Set in New Caledonia

Except in the United States of America, this book is sold subject to the
condition that it shall not, by way of trade or otherwise, be lent, re-sold,
hired out, or otherwise circulated without the publisher's prior consent
in any form of binding or cover other than that in which it is published
and without a similar condition including this condition being
imposed on the subsequent purchaser.

PENGUIN BOOKS

BLACK ODYSSEY

Mary Cable has contributed numerous short stories and non-fiction articles to *The New Yorker*, *Harper's Bazaar*, *The Atlantic*, *McCall's*, and other magazines, including *American Heritage*, where she has also been a member of the editorial staff. Mrs. Cable has traveled widely, having lived abroad for twelve years in four different countries while her husband was in the foreign service.

WITH LOVE, TO ARTHUR

ACKNOWLEDGMENTS

Thanks and appreciation are due to Dr. Robert Arthur Brent for permission to read his doctoral thesis, "Nicholas Philip Trist: Biography of a Disobedient Diplomat"; to James E. Daniels, Esq., for helping me understand certain aspects of state, federal, and admiralty law; to Warren Marr II and Dr. Clifton H. Johnson for allowing me to use the American Missionary Association archives; and to my sister, Elizabeth Pratt Holthusen, for loyal help in reading countless antique newspapers.

CONTENTS

1.	*The Black Schooner*	3
2.	*Kidnappers or Kidnapped?*	18
3.	*Lions of the Day*	33
4.	*The Prisoners' Story*	44
5.	*"It Is a National Matter"*	56
6.	*On Trial in New Haven*	67
7.	*Mr. Adams Takes the Case*	76
8.	*"This Most Singular Case"*	87
9.	*Verdict*	100
10.	*Light for the Dark Continent*	109
11.	*Missionaries and Amistads*	125
12.	*The End of the Odyssey*	134

Afterword	151
Appendix I: From *A History of the Amistad Captives* by John W. Barber (1840).	159
Appendix II: The *Antelope* Case	169
Bibliography	175
Index	179

BLACK ODYSSEY

1

THE BLACK SCHOONER

SOMETHING LIKE A PIRATE, announced a New York *Globe* headline on an August morning of 1839:

> The pilot boat *Blossom*, on Wednesday last off the Woodlands, fell in with a Baltimore-built schooner of about 150 tons, painted black with a white streak, two gilded stars on her stern, having on board apparently 25 or 30 men, all blacks, who requested something to eat and drink. The *Blossom* supplied them with water and bread. The next day took them in tow, when they attempted to board the pilot boat, which, to escape, cut the hawser. There were no persons on board that could speak English, and they appeared well supplied with cutlasses, but what their intentions were could not be understood.

So began a strange series of events that was to bedevil the diplomatic relations of the United States, Spain, and England for a generation; intensify bitterness over the question of slavery; and, at one of its most dramatic points, lead an ex-President of the United States to go before the Supreme Court

[3

and castigate the administration then in office. Because of the mysterious schooner and its black crew, thousands of white Americans turned their thoughts to Africa and, with pangs of conscience, felt an urgent need to send it missionaries instead of slave traders. Africa has not been quite the same since that August morning of 1839; nor, in a small but significant way, has America.

The *Globe* story aroused a lively interest. The public was not accustomed to any such excitement as a shipload of black men with cutlasses. Pirates were a thing of the past, at least in the North Atlantic. Slavers never ventured into coastal waters, for the slave trade had been outlawed since 1808. And the country had been at peace for twenty-five years. It had been a dull summer for news, with nothing much to put into headlines beyond occasional trouble with Indians on the faraway frontier. Martin Van Buren was in the third year of his presidency, with pre-election fervor still many months in the future.

During the second and third weeks of August, the newspapers made much of the mysterious schooner, long, low, and black, that continued to make *Flying Dutchman*–like appearances along the coast. Several ships reported having seen her in the distance, a strange apparition with tattered sails, a green bottom, no flag, and no apparent destination.

On August 20 the schooner *Emmeline*, out of New Bedford, sighted the stranger off Barnegat Bay and came alongside her. According to the *Emmeline*'s captain, the lettering on her stern appeared to read "*Hempsted*." She carried fore-topsail, with the rest of her sails blown to pieces. The captain counted twenty-five nearly naked black men on the deck. Some of these indicated by signs that they were out of drinking water and in a state of starvation. The *Emmeline* took the schooner in tow, but, when the black men armed themselves with sugar-cane knives and cutlasses, cast her off again. Shortly thereafter, seven of the armed blacks came alongside in a boat, asking for water. The captain told them to go back and get their papers. They did not return. An hour or so later, the crew of the *Emmeline* noticed a white man on the schooner's deck, but darkness fell before he could be observed closely. The next day, the *Emmeline* sighted the ship again, about eight miles away, firing three guns.

"The crew had a very savage appearance," the *Emmeline*'s captain later reported, "and the white man supposed to be the captain had a piratical look with a large moustache."

In New York the Collector of the Port dispatched a cutter to look for the strange ship and wrote to his counterpart in Boston, advising him to do the same. The steam frigate *Fulton*—the only steam vessel in the United States Navy— was also pressed into service, but since she could carry only enough fuel for four days, she was unable to venture far from New York harbor. A day or two later, another pilot boat arrived at New York with a report of a peculiarly acting ship that had a large eagle on her bow and a name that looked like *Almeda*.

On the morning of Monday, August 26, a bright, warm morning, two sea captains of Sag Harbor, Long Island— Henry Green and Peletiah Fordham—were shooting birds among the dunes of Long Island's eastern tip. To their astonishment, they came suddenly face to face with four black men, naked except for blankets. After a moment of consternation on both sides, a conversation of sorts was begun, by means of sign language and a few key words such as *America* and *Africa*. The blacks made it clear that they would like to know what country they were in and whether its people were slaveowners. On being assured that Long Island was not slave country, they led the two captains to the top of the dunes and pointed out a ship lying at anchor a mile or so to the north of the beach. She was a long, low, black schooner with an eagle on her bow, her sails in tatters, and no flag.

A boat was drawn up on the beach, guarded by several more black men. Some of them wore blankets, some merely bandannas tied around their loins, and one nothing but a white coat. But what Green and Fordham noticed in particular was that most of them sported necklaces and bracelets made of gold doubloons. The black who appeared to be the leader, a striking and very strong-looking young man, wore a necklace that, as Green afterward said, looked as if it were made of at least three hundred coins. When asked where these trinkets came from, the leader indicated that there were many more doubloons aboard the ship—two trunkfuls, in fact—and that these would belong to anyone who would get them provisions and then help them sail the ship to their home in Africa.

Captains Green and Fordham said later that they suspected things were "not right." They also soon realized that they were not the only Long Islanders to have encountered the strangers, for in a few minutes a party of blacks returned from a foraging expedition, bringing with them a loaf of bread, a bottle of gin, and two dogs, which they had bought from farmers and paid for royally with doubloons. Green suggested that the Africans go at once and get their trunks and bring them to the beach. After that, he told them, he would sail the ship to Africa.

Some of the blacks rowed back to the ship and presently returned with two heavy, rattling trunks and more of their companions, making the total number on the beach about twenty. At this juncture, a brig of the United States Coast Guard, the *Washington*, hove in sight off Gardiners Point. Green and Fordham, whose intention it was to take the ship into Sag Harbor and claim salvage rights to her, were considerably annoyed to see the *Washington* come about and lower a boat. The black men on shore piled hastily into their own boat and tried to get back to the schooner, but on the way they were intercepted by the boat from the brig, which was armed, and taken prisoner. The brig's commander, Lieutenant Gedney, lost no time in boarding the rattletrap schooner. After ordering all hands below at pistol point, Gedney proceeded, with caution, to look for "the piratical-looking white captain with a large moustache," of whom he had read in the newspapers. Suddenly an elderly white man, tattered, bearded, and sobbing, burst out upon the deck and threw his arms around Gedney's neck. He spoke only Spanish, but a minute later another Spaniard appeared from below, a young man who, it developed, had been educated in Connecticut and spoke fluent Yankee English. He lost no time in pouring out an extraordinary story.

The ship was the *Amistad* ("Friendship"), bound out of Havana for the Cuban coastal town of Puerto Príncipe. She had sailed on June 28 with five white men aboard—the captain and owner, Ramón Ferrer; the older man, Pedro Montes; the younger, José Ruiz; and two sailors. Besides these, there was a mulatto cook and a black cabin boy, Antonio, both the property of Captain Ferrer; four child slaves belonging to Montes—three little girls and a boy; and forty-nine male adult slaves, belonging to Ruiz. Montes and Ruiz had just bought their slaves in Havana and were returning with them to their homes in Príncipe, along with an agreeable cargo that included such things as silks, cottons, lace, looking glasses, books, bridles, saddles, pictures, fruit, olives, and wine, as well as a generous supply of gold doubloons.

On the fourth night at sea, the slaves had somehow managed to free themselves from their irons and had killed the

[7

captain and the cook. The two white crewmen had gone over the side in the stern boat. Montes had been wounded and in order to save his life had revealed that he understood navigation and could sail the ship to Africa. Ruiz was spared, apparently in order to help with the ship.

By making deliberately slow progress eastward during the day, and by sailing due westward under cover of night, Montes had hoped to reach the southern coast of the United States. Whenever he sighted another ship, he purposely put the *Amistad* on an erratic course, hoping to attract attention; but no one paid heed. In the Bahamas, the anchor was lowered several times and some of the blacks went ashore for water, taking care to select deserted islands. After more than six weeks at sea, the *Amistad* arrived where the *Washington* found her.

While Ruiz was telling this story, the leader of the Africans suddenly bounded from below through the main hatch and leaped over the side. He was naked except for his splendid necklace. The boat from the *Washington* put after him immediately, but whenever it came near him, he would dive like a seal and come up some distance away. This went on for nearly an hour. Then, exhausted, he took off his necklace and let it sink into the Atlantic—to his pursuers' considerable chagrin. After that he allowed himself to be recaptured. Lieutenant Gedney threw him in irons, and, having put the *Washington* in charge of the first mate, Lieutenant Meade, sent her to New London with the schooner in tow. He himself took a steamboat across Long Island Sound, arriving in New London ahead of his ship.

The Northern press made much of the *Amistad* story. (Southern papers avoided news of this sort, fearing to put ideas into the minds of the slave population.) THE PIRATE TAKEN, reported the New Haven *Daily Herald*:

Our information is imperfect, but this is no doubt the vessel reported sometime since to have sailed from Havana with a number of slaves on board and several white families to whom the slaves belonged. The blacks rose upon the whites and murdered them all—men, women, and children—to the number of 26 persons and took possession of the vessel and the valuable effects on board. We shall know more about them in a day or two.

What the *Herald* found out in a day or two was that its information was mostly wrong. Having sent no reporter to New London, the *Herald*—and nearly every other paper in the North—reprinted all or part of a long report from the New London *Gazette*, whose man had been waiting when the two ships appeared in New London harbor and had gone aboard along with the officials of the port and the medical officers. Nothing so exciting had ever happened in this quiet old port before, and the *Gazette* reporter made the most of it.

He wrote that the boarding party gave the *Amistad* a thorough inspection, gamely ignoring the appalling stench of her hold and deck. Ten of the Negroes had died, and others were sick. The schooner had been at sea sixty-three days, and her expensive cargo was scattered everywhere, "all mixed up in a strange and fantastic medley." Some of the blacks, "in a state of nudity, emaciated to mere skeletons, lay coiled upon the decks," while others stood about dressed in bits and pieces of finery.

> Here could be seen a negro with white pantaloons and the sable shirt which nature gave him, and a planter's broad brimmed hat upon his head, with a string of gewgaws about his neck; and another with a linen cambric shirt, whose bosom was worked by the hand of some dark-eyed daughter of Spain, while his nether proportions were enveloped in a shawl of gauze or Canton crepe. Around the

> windlass were gathered the three little girls, from eight to thirteen years of age, the very images of health and gladness. . . . On the forward hatch we unconsciously rested our hand on a cold object, which we soon discovered to be a naked corpse, enveloped in a pall of black bombazine. On removing its folds we beheld the rigid countenance and glazed eye of a poor negro who died last night. His mouth was unclosed and still wore the ghastly expression of his last struggle. Near by him, like some watching fiend, sat the most horrible creature we ever saw in human shape, an object of terror to the very blacks, who said that he was a cannibal. His teeth projected at almost right angles from his mouth, while the eyes had a most savage and demoniac expression.

Back aboard the *Washington*, the reporter interviewed Pedro Montes, who, he wrote, was

> the most striking instance of complacency and unalloyed delight we have ever witnessed, and it is not strange, since only yesterday his sentence was pronounced by the chief of the buccaneers, and his death song chanted by the grim crew, who gathered with uplifted sabres around his devoted head. . . . Every now and then he clasps his hands and with uplifted eyes gives thanks to "the Holy Virgin" who had led him out of his troubles.

After the initial excitement caused by the "pirate," with her tattered sails and green bottom, uncertainty began to beset the New London officials, the press, and the thoughtful public. Obviously, a crime had been committed and punishment should ensue. But what was the crime, who had committed it, and who should mete out the punishment? It fell to the United States District Attorney for Connecticut, William S. Holabird, to make an immediate decision; the schooner couldn't just lie there, with its sick and sorry crew. Holabird was an appointee of Martin Van Buren, a President known as "the Northerner with Southern sentiments." Holabird's personal sympathies lay entirely with Ruiz and Montes, but because the case was unprecedented he decided that he ought to write to the Secretary of State for instructions.

While awaiting an answer, he ordered a judicial hearing to be held immediately on board the *Washington*. This was not because he thought there were two sides to the case but because, as a representative of the law, it seemed suitable to him to put the matter into legal channels, especially since Lieutenant Gedney and the crew of the *Washington* were claiming salvage rights. The *Amistad* and her cargo were said to be worth forty thousand dollars, exclusive of the Negroes, whose value on the Havana market was estimated at between twenty and thirty thousand dollars. Holabird felt that such an important matter should be decided in court. He had no notion, of course, that the repercussions of what seemed to him a simple and logical step would be felt for the next thirty years.

Holabird was no doubt glad that the hearing fell under the jurisdiction of Andrew T. Judson, a judge of the District Court of Connecticut. Like Holabird, Judson was a Van Buren appointee and no friend of the black man. In 1833, he had been the prosecuting attorney in the famous case of Prudence Crandall versus the State of Connecticut. Miss Crandall, a schoolmistress of Canterbury, Connecticut, had taken Negro children into her school. When the townspeople protested, she had turned the school into one for Negroes only, some of whom came from other states to board with her. The state brought suit. Judson, as prosecutor, contended that she had violated a Connecticut law (enacted not long before at the instigation of Judson) that concerned "admission and settlement of inhabitants in towns" and was designed to prevent

Negroes from moving into the state. The defense held that such a law was unconstitutional. Judson argued that Negroes are not citizens within the meaning of that term as used in the Constitution. Said he, "It was far from the intention [of the founding fathers] to include blacks under the term 'citizen.'" The jury had been unable to agree. So had the Supreme Court of Connecticut and the Court of Errors. Thereupon, the peaceful Yankees of Canterbury suddenly spawned a mob that set fire to Prudence Crandall's house and, when Miss Crandall and her girls put out the fire, invaded it and pulled it to pieces. At this point, fearing for her own life and those of her pupils, Miss Crandall gave up her school.

This had been Connecticut's only case of mob violence in connection with the Negro question. As Holabird knew, the state contained a good many abolitionists, as did neighboring New York and Massachusetts; and he was anxious to get the *Amistad*'s mutineers out and away before anyone tried to make heroes of them.

On the morning of August 29, aboard the *Washington* in New London harbor, the judicial hearing was opened by His Honor Judge Judson. Don Pedro Montes and Don José Ruiz lodged a complaint against the mutineers, listing their names as they appeared in the *Amistad*'s papers: Joseph Cinquez, Antonio Simón, Lucas, José, Pedro, Martín, Manuel, Andrés, Eduardo, Celedonio, Bártolo, Ramón, Agustín, Evanisto, Casimiro, Melchior, Gabriel, Santorion, Escolástico, Pascual, Estanislao, Desiderio, Nícolo, Esteban, Tomás, Cosme, Luis, Julian, Federico, Salustiano, Ladislao, Celestino, Epifaneo, Tuburcio, Venducio, Felipe, Hipólito, Venito, Isidoro, Vicinte, Dionisio, Apoloneo, Esequiel, León, Julio, Hipólito, and Zenon—"or such of the above as might be alive." When it was found that none of the Africans answered to these names, heads were counted, and "Joseph Cinquez" and thirty-eight others were found to be present. It was a mystery which Spanish name belonged to which.

After the reading of their alleged names, all were indicted for murder and piracy, and their leader, "Joseph Cinquez," was brought before the court (the others remaining in the brig). His African name, phonetically spelled, appears to have been "Singbe-pieh," but the newspapers of the time variously called him Cinquez, Sinko, Jingua, and Cinque. We will call him Cinque, as that eventually became the most usual version.

Cinque was wearing a red flannel shirt, white duck pants, and manacles. "His appearance was neat," said the New Haven *Daily Herald,* which had its own reporter present, "and in cleanliness would compare advantageously with any colored dandy on Broadway." Another reporter, sympathetic to the mutineers, wrote:

> This Cinquez is one of those spirits who appear but seldom. Possessing far more sagacity and courage than his race generally do, he had been accustomed to command. . . . His lips are thicker and more turned up than those of his race in general, but when opened display a set of teeth rivalling in beauty the most regular of those which we praise so much in Caucasian beauty. But his nostrils are the most remarkable feature he possesses. These he can contract or dilate at pleasure. His general deportment is free from levity and many white men might take a lesson in dignity and forebearance from the African Chieftain. . . .

Cinque did not seem frightened, and even gave an occasional melancholy smile. Once or twice he made a motion with his hand on his throat, to suggest hanging. Not understanding a word of the proceedings, he remained a mute though attentive spectator.

The *Amistad*'s papers were produced. Among them were licenses, issued under the printed name of the Governor of Havana, assigning three slaves to Pedro Montes and forty-nine to Señor Ruiz. There were also passports for the whites, one for the mulatto slave, Antonio, and a collective one for all fifty-two Africans. The passports gave permission for the schooner and those aboard her to proceed from Havana to Puerto Príncipe.

Lieutenant Meade, first mate of the *Washington*, who spoke Spanish and was serving the court as interpreter for Montes, testified that when he and Gedney had boarded the *Amistad*, Señores Ruiz and Montes had handed over the ship's papers to him and claimed protection, which, of course, had been immediately provided. Señor Ruiz was now sworn and testified as follows: He had gone to Havana, purchased forty-nine slaves, and loaded them on board the schooner. For the first four days all was well. On the fourth night he was awakened by noises and realized that a mutiny was in progress, though there was no moon and it was too dark to see what was going on. He did, however, see "Joseph" (Cinque): "I took an oar and tried to quell the mutiny; I cried no! no! I then heard one of the crew cry murder. I then heard the captain order the cabin boy to go below and get some bread to throw among the negroes, hoping to pacify them. I did not see the captain killed.

"They called me on deck and told me I should not be hurt. I asked them as a favor to spare the old man [Montes]. They did so. After this they went below and ransacked the trunks of the passengers. Before doing this they tied our hands. We all slept on deck. The next day the slaves told me that they had killed only the captain and cook. The other two [sailors] had escaped in a small boat.

"The cabin boy is an African by birth but has lived a long time in Cuba. His name is Antonio and [he] belonged to the captain. From this time we were compelled to steer east in the day; but sometimes the wind would not allow us to steer east, then they would threaten us with death. In the night we steered west and kept to the northward as much as possible. We were six or seven leagues* from the land when the outbreak took place. Antonio is yet alive—they would have killed him but he acted as interpreter. . . ."

Ruiz testified in English, but old Señor Montes, who was sworn in next, spoke in Spanish, which was translated by Lieutenant Meade: "We left Havana on the 28th of June. I owned four slaves, three females and one male. [This statement differs from the data in the ship's papers, which assign to Montes three girl slaves only—"Juana," "Francisca," and "Josefa."] For three days the wind was ahead and all went well. Between 11 and 12 at night, just as the moon was rising, sky dark and cloudy, weather very rainy, on the fourth night, I lay down on a mattress. Between 3 and 4 was awakened by a noise which was caused by blows given to the mulatto cook. I went on deck and they attacked me. I seized a stick and a knife with a view to defend myself. I did not wish to kill or hurt them. At this time the prisoner wounded me on the head severely with one of the sugar knives, also on the arm. I then ran below and stowed myself between two barrels, wrapped up in a sail. The prisoner rushed after me and attempted to kill me, but was prevented by the interference of another man. I recollect who struck me, but was not sufficiently sensible to distinguish the man who saved me. I was faint from loss of blood. I then was taken on deck and tied to the hand of Ruiz. After this they commanded us to steer for their country. I told them I did not know the way. I was much afraid, and had lost my senses, so I cannot recollect who tied me.

* One league equals three miles.

"On the second day after the mutiny a heavy gale came on. I still steered, having once been master of a vessel. When recovered, I steered for Havana in the night by the stars, but by the sun in the day, taking care to make no more way than possible. After sailing fifty leagues, we saw an American merchant ship, but did not speak her. We were also passed by a schooner, but were unnoticed. Every moment my life was threatened. I know nothing of the murder of the captain. All I know of the murder of the mulatto is that I heard the blows. He was asleep when attacked. Next morning the negroes had washed the decks. They were all glad, next day, at what had happened. The prisoner treated me harshly and but for the interference of others, would have killed me several times every day. We kept no reckoning. I did not know how many days we had been out, nor what day of the week it was when the officers came on board. We anchored at least thirty times, and lost an anchor at New Providence. When at anchor we were treated well, but at sea they acted very cruelly toward me. They once wanted me to drop anchor in the high seas. I had no wish to kill any of them, but prevented them from killing each other."

At this point Judge Judson might well have ordered the ship to be handed over to the Spanish consul at Boston, as Montes and Ruiz were requesting. But Lieutenant Gedney and Lieutenant Meade were concerned with their salvage rights, and feared that if the *Amistad* sailed back to Havana, they would hear no more of her. Ruiz and Montes, indeed, had declared their belief that as officers of the Coast Guard, Gedney and his men had merely been performing their duty and were entitled to no compensation other than gratitude. With this the two Spaniards were generous, even taking the trouble to insert a notice of thanks in the New London *Gazette*.

Perhaps only because of the salvage question, but perhaps

also because of some apprehension that the matter was not as simple as it looked, Judge Judson referred the case for trial by the Circuit Court, meanwhile remanding all the defendants to the custody of the United States Marshal. As the New London jail was wanting in facilities for so large a crowd, the prisoners were sent by water to New Haven, where they were lodged in the county jail. Cinque, who was regarded as dangerous, was brought separately and kept in irons. Neither he nor his companions could make any sense out of what was going on, and they lived in terror. They were aware that the death penalty in Havana was either burning at the stake or hanging; and, for all they knew, the same might apply in New England.

2

KIDNAPPERS OR KIDNAPPED?

Congress was in recess when the newspapers began to report the *Amistad* mutiny, and a certain venerable Congressman, John Quincy Adams, read about it at his peaceful family homestead in Quincy, Massachusetts. He wrote in his diary, "That which now absorbs a great part of my time and all my good feelings is the case of 53 African negroes taken at sea off Montauk. . . ." He believed they had a just cause, and when he read a letter in the newspaper written in their behalf by William Jay, son of the nation's first Chief Justice, he wrote Jay privately to say he agreed. However, the matter was no direct concern of his and he had enough problems on his hands in Congress, where, at the age of seventy-two, having been President and Secretary of State, as well as a Senator, a Harvard professor, and several times United States minister to foreign countries, he was serving as Representative from the Plymouth district. "Prudence would forbid my giving an opinion upon [the case] at any time," he noted in his diary, "and if I ever do it must be with great consideration and self-controul."

The notion that any respectable citizen could have anything to say for the blacks did not, at first, occur to those in charge of them. Holabird had written to the Secretary of State describing an open-and-shut instance of murder and mutiny, in which Gedney had rescued the Spaniards from the blacks, not the blacks from the Spaniards. All concerned (except the Africans) were well aware of the movement called abolitionism, but considered its advocates to be nothing but a noisy parcel of fanatics. The 1830s had fostered protest movements of all kinds, and conventional men like Gedney and Holabird had no use for any of them. Transcendentalists, Mormons, Shakers, Fourierists, members of the Oneida or the Skaneateles communities, perfectionists, supporters of women's rights, and abolitionists—they were all regarded by the average citizen as mischievous fools.

Many Americans in 1839 were opposed to slavery, but by no means all of them thought that abolition, the immediate emancipation of all slaves, was the answer. Many, including slaveowners, contributed funds to the American Colonization Society, which sent shiploads of freed slaves to start their own state in Liberia. Others disliked slavery but believed that it was God's Will. Still others—John Quincy Adams was among them—feared that to oppose slavery would be to bring about a worse evil, the dissolution of the Union. Most people preferred not to think about it at all.

The abolitionists seized upon the *Amistad* case as heaven-sent to abet their cause. Until now, they had been handicapped by the fact that the objects of their concern were in the South, where they dared not venture. A governor of South Carolina spoke for Southern public opinion when he declared, "The laws of every community should punish this species of interference with death without benefit of clergy." There was even difficulty in sending abolitionist newspapers and pamphlets into the South. In 1835 bags full of undelivered antislavery literature were burned at Charleston, and the Postmaster General said that while he had no legal authority to permit such an action, he would not "recommend" delivery of antislavery mail. "We owe an obligation to the laws," said he, "but a higher one to the communities in which we live, and if the former be perverted to destroy the latter, it is patriotism to disregard them." The same year, President Jackson, in his annual message to Congress, asked for a law to prohibit these "incendiary publications" from entering Southern states. A committee, of which John Calhoun was chairman, recommended that the states themselves should decide what they considered incendiary; each state should pass its own law on the matter, and the federal government would "give effect" to such state laws. A bill making it illegal "for any postmaster to deliver material touching on slavery in states where such circulation is prohibited" was defeated in the Senate by a small margin. In the end there was a sudden awakening to the fact that tampering with the mail was unconstitutional, and a law was passed requiring postal officials to deliver anything committed to their charge. Nevertheless, they frequently failed to do so.

But antislavery literature did not free slaves. Until the *Amistad* Africans arrived in Connecticut, the abolitionists could do little except hold meetings and recruit members in the North. Their meetings were sometimes attacked by mobs. In 1833 a meeting in New York was broken up, and Arthur Tappan, one of the abolitionist leaders, was attacked by a man with a dagger. The following year another meeting was disrupted by a mob that then continued to rampage through the streets of Manhattan for several days, while the newspapers rampaged against Arthur Tappan. Tappan's drygoods store, the largest in New York, was attacked; Tappan closed the iron shutters and armed his clerks with muskets. His brother Lewis, also a leading abolitionist, suffered damages to his house in Rose Street. In the South, fifty thousand dollars were offered for the head of each Tappan brother. "If that sum is placed in a New York bank," said Arthur, "I may possibly think of giving myself up." Insurance companies refused to insure the Tappans' property. Threatening letters came continually. Someone in the South sent Arthur a slave's ear in a box. On one occasion a tender belonging to a United States Revenue cutter arrived in New York harbor from Charleston, South Carolina, carrying eighteen men who proposed to kidnap the Tappans.

The mother of Arthur and Lewis Tappan who was a greatniece of a former president of the Pennsylvania Abolitionist Society—Benjamin Franklin. One of their brothers, Benjamin, later became a Senator from Ohio and an Associate Justice of the Supreme Court; he too was an abolitionist. A fourth brother, John, made a large fortune as a businessman in Boston, and did not share his brothers' enthusiasms. Arthur and Lewis also made fortunes, from which they gave generously to causes: besides the Antislavery Society, they were both active in the American Sunday School Union, the American Bible Society, the American Tract Society, the Union Missionary Society, the American Education Society, the New York Magdalen Society, and the General Union for Promoting the Observance of the Christian Sabbath. When the American Colonization Society was first started, in 1816, Arthur and Lewis had supported that, too. But they later came to believe that it was inefficient and that the scheme was unworkable. They agreed with Daniel Webster, who, when asked to help establish a

Massachusetts branch of the society, said, "Gentlemen, I will have nothing more to do with the matter; for I am satisfied it is merely a plan of the slaveholders to get rid of the free negroes." Henry Clay, a large slaveholder, made no bones about his reason for supporting colonization. He said he hoped it would "rid our country of a useless and pernicious if not dangerous portion of its population."

When William Lloyd Garrison started the abolitionist paper *The Liberator*, Arthur Tappan helped underwrite it. The following year, 1832, Arthur bought some land in New Haven with the plan of using it for a college for Negroes. But a New Haven town meeting decided that "the establishment of a college to educate the colored people is incompatible with the prosperity if not the existence of the present institution of learning, and destructive to the best interests of the city." Both Arthur and Lewis gave money to the newly founded Oberlin College, which took Negro students. Arthur paid for Prudence Crandall's defense, while Lewis offered to give five thousand dollars to the Bible Society if it would distribute five thousand free Bibles to Negroes. The Bible Society refused.

It was Lewis Tappan who first came to the rescue of the Africans of the *Amistad*. As soon as he read of the case, he summoned a meeting in New York of leading abolitionists. His brother Arthur was away in England, but to the meeting came Joshua Leavitt, editor of the abolitionist paper *The Emancipator;* Simeon Jocelyn, white pastor of a Negro church in New Haven; William Jay, whose father, Chief Justice and Vice President John Jay, had once been president of the New York Manumission Society; and a number of other able and dedicated citizens. At last they had an opportunity to take action in behalf of slaves, slaves who were right here in the supposedly free North, not out of reach in the South.

They formed the Committee for the Defense of the Africans of the *Amistad*, and immediately sent letters to the papers appealing for funds and legal assistance.

Meanwhile, the Spanish minister at Washington, Señor Angel Calderón de la Barca, had been apprised of the situation, and on September 6 he sent a long letter about it to Mr. John Forsyth, the Secretary of State. Calderón and Forsyth met often in Washington society, where they were both regarded as particularly elegant and charming gentlemen. Forsyth had been minister to Spain from 1819 to 1823. He had also served in Congress and as Governor of Georgia, and had been appointed Secretary of State by Andrew Jackson in 1834. At that time he had tried to get the post of minister to Russia, remarking that he would "be able to satisfy our European friends that it is possible for an American minister to have the manner and look of a gentleman." Although a Jacksonian, he had little use for the masses and certainly none at all for Negroes, except as slaves. Aware of this, Señor Calderón must have felt confident that the *Amistad* matter would be settled at once. Had he known that his letter of September 6 would be the first in an exchange of notes on the subject that would go on for more than twenty years, he might not have written so calmly and with such exquisite courtesy.

First, he reviewed the circumstances of the mutiny and of the capture by the brig *Washington*. "The act of humanity thus performed," he wrote, "would have been complete had the vessel at the same time been set at liberty, and the negroes sent to be tried by the proper tribunal, and by the violated laws of the country of which they are subjects." But, alas, things had begun to go wrong in New London. An "incompetent tribunal" had got hold of the case; the officers of the *Washington* had claimed salvage rights; and the ship, cargo, and Negroes had been detained. (That Calderón distinguished between "cargo" and "Negroes" was a point to be made much of later on.) The Spanish government, therefore, now requested Mr. Forsyth to have the vessel delivered up to her Cuban owners without any salvage being paid; that he declare that no tribunal in the United States had jurisdiction over subjects of Spain; and that he order the Negroes to be sent to Havana "in order to their being tried by the Spanish laws which they have violated; and that in the meantime they be kept in safe custody, in order to prevent their evasion; and that if in consequence of the intervention of the authorities of Connecticut there should be any delay in the desired delivery of the vessel and the slaves, the owners both of the latter and of the former be indemnified for the injury that may accrue to them."

In support of his request, Señor Calderón cited three articles of a treaty signed in 1795 between the United States and Spain. Since the bearing of these articles on the *Amistad* case was to be debated over and over again, it might be well to get them in mind (the italics are Señor Calderón's):

Article 8: In case the subjects and inhabitants of either party, with their shipping, whether public and of war, or private and of merchants, be forced, through stress of weather, *pursuit of pirates or enemies, or any other urgent necessity* for seeking of shelter and harbor, to retreat and enter into any of the rivers, bays, roads, or ports, belonging to the other party, they shall be received and treated with all humanity, and enjoy all favor, protection and help; and they shall be permitted to refresh and provide themselves, *at reasonable rates,* with victuals and all things needful for the subsistence of their persons, or reparation of their ships, and prosecution of their voyage; and *they shall no ways be hindered from returning out of said ports* or roads, but may remove and depart when and whither they please without any let or hindrance.

Article 9: All ships and merchandise, of what nature soever, which shall be rescued out of the hands of any pirates or robbers on the high seas, shall be brought into some port of either State, and shall be delivered to the custody of the officers of that port, in order *to be taken care of, and restored entire* to the true proprietor, as soon as due and sufficient proof shall be made concerning the property thereof.

Article 10: When any vessel of either party shall be wrecked, foundered, or otherwise damaged, on the coasts or within the dominion of the other, their respective subjects or citizens shall receive as well for themselves as for their vessels and effects, *the same assistance which would be due to the inhabitants of the country where the damage happens, and shall pay the same charges and dues only as the said inhabitant would be subject to pay in a like case;* and if the operations of repair should require that the whole or any part of the cargo be unladen, they shall pay no duties, charges, or fees, on the part which they shall relade and carry away.

The Spanish minister went on to point out that if the *Amistad* mutineers were to go unpunished, there might be further slave revolts in Cuba, "where the citizens of the United States not only carry on a considerable trade, but where they possess territorial properties which they cultivate with the labor of African slaves"; and that even if the "incompetent tribunal" in Connecticut should try the Negroes and condemn them to death, the "salutary effects" would not be the same as if the case were to be decided in Cuba. The people of Cuba and Puerto Rico would live in dread of slave insurrections, "and in lieu of the harmony and good feeling subsisting between them and the citizens of the United States it would not be surprising . . . if sentiments were awakened of a different nature.

The rest of Señor Calderón's letter was devoted to a denunciation of abolitionists. "No one," he wrote, "is ignorant of the existence of a considerable number of persons who . . . are employing all the means which knowledge and wealth can afford for effecting, at any price, the emancipation of the slaves." Calderón knew little or nothing about the Tappan brothers, but the description fitted them perfectly. Even while he was writing his letter, the *Amistad* committee was lining up the best possible legal advice for the defense of the Africans.

There was nothing either mercenary or fly-by-night about the lawyers who volunteered in their defense. Roger Baldwin, of New Haven, was the son of a well-known jurist and governor of Connecticut, while his grandfather had been a prominent Revolutionary patriot. Theodore Sedgwick was the son of a leading New York lawyer. Seth Staples, of New Haven, was the future founder of the Yale Law School. The Governor of Connecticut, William Ellsworth, also offered to appear as a lawyer for the defense, but when he found he was too late, he decided—rather surprisingly—to represent the Sag Harbor sea captain, Henry Green, in his salvage claims.

The defense was to be based on a fact that was probably unknown to Judge Judson and District Attorney Holabird and that Secretary Forsyth and His Excellency Señor Calderón had chosen to forget: nineteen years previously, England, having freed her own slaves, had paid Spain four hundred thousand pounds on condition that slavery would be made illegal in Spain and her colonies. Under the terms of the treaty, no new slaves could be imported into Spanish territory. Persons already in slavery were to remain slaves, but their children born after 1820, the year of the treaty, were to be taught a trade and set free when they were old enough to pursue it. The treaty, which was reaffirmed in 1835, allowed the British to maintain observers in Havana to see that it was honored. Thus (said the *Amistad* committee), according to the laws of Spain herself, the Africans of the *Amistad* had been brought to Cuba illegally, and Ruiz and Montes were not their masters but their kidnappers. In mutinying, the Africans had merely defended their rights as free men.

The Spanish antislavery law, however, was one in name only. Few citizens of either Spain or Cuba even knew that it existed; those who did regarded it as a good joke on the British. The fact that the *Amistad* slaves were fresh from Africa was of no interest to Ruiz, who readily admitted that he knew it but insisted that since he had bought and paid for them he had a legal right to them.

The point was debated at length in the newspapers. A letter to the editor of the New York *Daily Express* inquired:

> If Tom Nokes should steal your horse and sell him in the open horse market to Dick Stiles, would such sale give Dick a legal right to your horse and be a sufficient bar to your recovery? Ruiz . . . bought the legal right of the slave trader—who had none, and of course could transfer none.

To which the *Express* replied:

> If Dick Stiles bought a stolen horse, Dick has a prima facie legal right of possession till the owner proves a better one. If Dick's prima facie horse runs away with Dick, into Richard Roe's pasture, Dick has a right to claim that the question of ownership be settled in his village and not by Richard's household. If Dick admitted he bought the horse of a supposed thief, can't Dick offset his admission by cer-

tificates which show the government sanctioned the robbery? We admit this is a *questio vexata*—an excellent one to puzzle legal heads with.

Before the trial, which was to begin in Hartford on September 17, the all-important task of the *Amistad* committee was to discover what language the Africans spoke and then find an interpreter. Antonio, the cabin boy, understood the prisoners only slightly, and was, anyway, completely distrusted by them. As soon as the first appeal for funds and legal help had been published, the committee delegated Joshua Leavitt to go to New Haven, taking with him an old African-born free Negro who spoke a language of the Congo.

Leavitt found New Haven in an uproar. As many as five thousand people daily were thronging to the county jail, which overlooked the Green. The jailer, Colonel Pendleton, was charging "one New York shilling" (twelve and a half cents) for a look at the Africans. "Great curiosity is felt," Leavitt wrote, "to see these victims of the slave trade, the first that have been known in Connecticut for a great many years." The victims (or villains) were occupying "four or five apartments," except for Cinque, who was in irons and confined among the jail's regular complement of criminals. Leavitt felt that they were being treated humanely, except that they lacked fresh air and opportunity for exercise. They had all been provided with shirts and trousers. The weather had been very warm during the week of their capture, but on August 30 the temperature had plummeted from ninety degrees to fifty-three, and a severe storm had torn off roofs and uprooted trees all over New England. The Africans, unaccustomed either to cool weather or to clothes, may not have minded staying inside. "They all appear to be persons of quiet minds and a mild and cheerful temper," reported Leavitt. "There are no contentions among them; even the poor children, three girls and a boy, who are in a room by themselves, seem to be uniformly kind and friendly. Joseph Cinquez . . . is less cheerful than many of the others."

The old man from the Congo was unable to communicate with any of them. Some identified themselves as "Mandingo," * but Leavitt felt sure that they were not all from one tribe. "Unremitting efforts will be made to obtain the means of communication with these unfortunate persons who have been committed to prison and bound over to be tried for their lives, without an opportunity to say a word for themselves, and without a word communicated to them explanatory of their situation."

A day or two later, Lewis Tappan joined Leavitt in New Haven. He was shocked by the circusy atmosphere surrounding the jail, and got on the wrong side of Colonel Pendleton by asking him what he was going to do with all the money he was taking in. The colonel replied testily that it would go to buy clothing and other necessities for the prisoners, and that he would keep "a small amount" to compensate himself for the immense amount of trouble and extra work. Tappan was not allowed to visit Cinque, but spoke to him through an open door and understood him to say that his name was Shinequau. He was, said Tappan, "Wholly unclothed—a blanket partly wrapped around him. He does not seem to like the tight dress of this country."

Three of the prisoners died during September. Their disease, according to the New Haven doctors who examined them, was "white flux." The antislavery newspapers said that it was a result of their ill treatment aboard the slave ship coming from Africa, while the proslavery newspapers said that

* "Mandingo" signifies a division of Negro peoples of West Africa, comprising a large number of tribes.

they had obviously "made too free" with the *Amistad*'s edible cargo and, subsequently, with her medicine cabinet.

On the bright side, the jailer took the children to ride in a wagon, and Tappan reported that they looked "robust" and "full of hilarity." All except Cinque and those who were ill were now being brought out to the Green once or twice a day for exercise. Crowds gathered to watch them cavort, turn somersaults, and leap about as no adult New Englander would have dreamed of doing, thus re-enforcing the convictions of virtually everyone that theirs was a childlike race.

In spite of such antics, all the blacks except the children appeared apprehensive about their fate. One day a kindly clergyman who was visiting them brought several of them into a front room of the jail so that they might watch a militia review that was going on on the Green. The clergyman wrote later, "They all shrunk back, and directly inquired if preparations were making to cut their throats; and they were much frightened by some of the military who came into the jail with their swords, to visit them." They were also apprehensive (Cinque said later) about the numbers of clergymen who came to see them. They looked so solemn in their plain black clothes that the prisoners took them for judges or executioners.

Most of the visitors were curiosity seekers. A few were reporters, and one was a young artist, Simeon Jocelyn's younger brother, Nathaniel, who was allowed to paint Cinque's portrait. The owner of a waxworks museum, one Mr. Moulthrop, took life masks of the prisoners—a process that caused them great alarm—so that people who could not get to the jail might call at Moulthrop's and settle for Africans of black wax. A phrenologist, a Mr. Fletcher, had examined the prisoners while they were still on the *Amistad*, after going aboard with the port officials and the doctors. In those pre-

Freudian days, phrenology was believed by many to provide a serious gauge of personality (among the many was Queen Victoria, whose private phrenologist, George Combe, came to America the following year and made his own analysis of the *Amistad* prisoners). Even the skeptical regarded phrenology as more sensible than astrology or divination. Mr. Fletcher's findings were published in full by many newspapers, and he used them as the basis of a busy winter on the lecture platform.

"Cinque," Fletcher said, "appears to be about 26 years of age, of powerful frame, bilious and sanguine temperament, bilious predominating. His head by measurement is 22⅜ inches in circumference, 15 from the root of the nose to the occipital protuberance over the top of the head, 15 inches from the Meatus Auditorius to do [ditto] over the head, and 5¾ through the head at destructiveness.

"The development of the faculties is as follows: Firmness; Self-Esteem; Hope: —very large.

"Benevolence; Veneration; Conscientiousness; Approbativeness; Wonder; Concentrativeness; Inhabitiveness; Comparison; Form: —large.

"Amativeness; Philoprogenitiveness; Adhesiveness; Combativeness; Destructiveness; Secretiveness; Constructiveness; Caution; Language; Individuality; Eventuality; Causality; Order: —average.

"Alimentiveness; Acquisitiveness; Ideality; Mirthfulness; Imitation; Size; Weight; Color; Locality; Number; Time; Tune: —moderate and small."

"On the whole," said Fletcher, Cinque's head was "such as a phrenologist admires." His behavior during the mutiny and subsequently had been clearly dictated by his phrenological make-up, and was "a perfect illustration of the truth of the science."

As for the other prisoners, Fletcher found them well endowed with Benevolence and Hope. "One is said to be of the Caromnache tribe (man-eaters) but he denies, as well as I could understand, that he has ever eaten human flesh, and there is certainly far more destructiveness in the look of his mouth and protruding teeth than there is in his brain."

The suspected cannibal, who had so frightened the New London *Gazette* reporter on the deck of the *Amistad*, had turned out to be one of the gentlest and most amiable of the whole group. His name was Ko-no-ma. His long, tusklike teeth, it now appeared, were the result of lifelong teasing outward by means of some device producing an opposite effect from that of our children's braces. A doctor offered to pull them for him but he declined—"evidently prizing them very much," one of the clergymen reported. After Ko-no-ma had got over his initial bewilderment and fright, he often showed all his terrifying "tushes" in a friendly grin.

But what the Africans needed more than they needed either Mr. Fletcher or a dentist was an interpreter. The day of the trial was approaching rapidly and the defendants were still inarticulate.

3

LIONS OF THE DAY

Fortunately for the Africans, friends were close at hand in New Haven. At the Yale Divinity School, many of the professors and students regarded their arrival as a Special Providence, planned by the Lord for no less a purpose than to bring about the Christianization of Africa. Leonard Bacon, one of New England's most eminent divines and a colonizationist rather than an abolitionist, organized a committee of clergymen and theological students to visit the county jail every day and try to communicate with the prisoners. One clergyman, George E. Day, had formerly taught at the New York School for the Deaf and Dumb, and could apply to the project his valuable experience in difficult communication. Another, Dr. Josiah Willard Gibbs,* was a noted Hebrew scholar with a special interest in philology. Between them, Day and Gibbs established that the language spoken by most of the prisoners was Mende, and that they came from a region south and southeast of Freetown, in the British colony of

* The father of the eminent scientist Willard Gibbs.

Sierra Leone. Dr. Gibbs had the prisoners teach him how to count in Mende and then took himself off to the New York waterfronts, where he wandered up and down for several days, counting in Mende to every black man he met. A scholarly-looking clergyman of fifty, he must have been an unusual sight on the raffish docks of New York. He was beginning to grow discouraged by the blank stares he met and the amusement he seemed to cause, when he at last found a young Negro sailor from a British man-of-war, whose face lit up with pleasure when he heard "one-two-three-four-five-six-seven-eight-nine-ten" recited in Mende.

The sailor was John Ferry, a free Negro who had been born a Mende, kidnapped at an early age by enemy tribesmen, sold to a Portuguese slave trader, and rescued at sea by a British patrol vessel. Since then he had lived in Freetown. He said he understood Mende, although he had not used it for years. Dr. Gibbs spoke to the captain of Ferry's ship and was able to procure a leave of absence for him. As it turned out, Ferry was more willing than useful. His Mende was limited, but with his help the lawyers were able to get the gist of the African story of the mutiny.

After Judge Judson had referred the case to the Circuit Court, District Attorney Holabird wrote a second time to Secretary of State Forsyth. He was clearly uneasy about the matter. "The next term of our circuit court sits on the 17th instant, at which time I suppose it will be my duty to bring them to trial unless they are in some other way disposed of. Should you have any instructions to give on the subject, I should like to receive them as soon as may be." Three days later, he wrote again. He had been looking into the law more fully and now feared he had made a mistake in permitting the case to get into the courts. "I would respectfully inquire, sir, whether there are no treaty stipulations with the Government of Spain that would authorize our Government to deliver them up to the Spanish authorities; and, if so, whether it could be done before our court sits?"

On September 11, perhaps before receiving Holabird's second letter, Forsyth wrote to acknowledge receipt of the first. He said that the Spanish minister had requested immediate custody of the schooner, cargo, and slaves; and that he, Forsyth, had asked President Van Buren what to do. Gedney's demand for salvage rights was the complicating factor; otherwise, the Spanish request might well have been granted. "In the mean time," Forsyth wrote, "you will take care that no proceeding of your circuit court or of any other judicial tribunal, places the vessel, cargo, or slaves beyond the control of the Federal Executive." Here, of course, was the old story of stolen horse and locked barn door: the case was already beyond executive control.

Forsyth did not acknowledge Calderón's letter of September 6 until September 16. If ten days seems a long time to answer such an urgent letter as Señor Calderón's, it must be remembered that Mr. Forsyth had no idea what to say. His belated letter stated merely that he was awaiting President Van Buren's decision. Señor Calderón acknowledged the acknowledgment the next day. The President said nothing. Possibly his silence was the result of a letter he had received from two of the *Amistad* committee lawyers, Staples and Sedgwick, in which they said that (1) the Treaty of 1795 did not apply in this case because conflicting claims of property were involved; (2) the Negroes had been brought to Cuba against the laws of that country and against the provisions of the antislavery treaty between Spain and Great Britain; (3) under that law, Ruiz and Montes had no title to the Africans; and (4) the Negroes had "liberated themselves from illegal restraint." The letter added, "It is this question, sir, fraught

[35

with the deepest interest, that we pray you to submit for adjudication to the tribunals of the land. It is this question that we pray may not be decided in the recesses of the cabinet, where these unfriended men can have no counsel and can produce no proof, but in the halls of Justice, with the safeguards that she throws around the unfriended and oppressed."

President Van Buren did not answer this letter, but neither did he issue an executive order to hand the *Amistad* and its cargo back to the Spanish. And there the matter stood when the case came to court in Hartford.

On September 14 all the prisoners except one named Burna, who was very ill, were sent to Hartford. They traveled by canal boat as far as Farmington, and all along the canal the banks were thick with crowds waiting for a look at them. From Farmington to Hartford they went by stage directly to the county jail. A steamboat carrying reporters and officials bound for Hartford went aground in a fog along the canal at Weathersfield, and did not arrive until after dark. On board were Montes and Ruiz; Lewis Tappan and Theodore Sedgwick, Jr.; Lieutenant Meade; and an "iron-faced man from Philadelphia" who said he had once been in the slave trade, could speak Mende, and was coming to offer his services as interpreter. On such a small boat it must have been difficult for the antagonists to ignore each other—especially under the informal conditions of going aground.

A reporter from the New York *Express* filed a lively story from Hartford: "The abolitionists," he said, "have secured enough legal ability to delay anything til the end of the earth. . . . It is to be hoped that Señores Montes and Ruiz will have legal ability provided to match what the Africans have, in which case we shall have about as brilliant a tournament *in curia* as has happened this long while. . . ."

Ruiz called on his property in jail, the *Express* story went on. The property seemed glad to see him, although "Cinque drew his hand across his throat." The Cuban slave boy, Antonio, "leans his chair back against the wall of the prison, puts his feet in its rounds and then whistles away—in utter disregard of black and white around him. Antonio is a jolly boy." (Other reporters said that he acted "superior" and that his companions disliked him.) "All the blacks are on benches in a long train. Some squat like tailors. Some stretch out at full length and eat and sleep and sleep and eat. Some chatter away in a liquid lingo—displaying their pearly teeth of inimitable beauty between lips of undiluted black." The Philadelphia slave trader proved incomprehensible to the Africans. "Susoo, Mandingo, and Boolam are the languages now all the go. People here about may forget English soon and Mandingo be the language of the day."

There were a great many strangers in the city. The African captives were the center of attraction, and in three days three thousand persons visited them in the jail. "One man," said the Hartford *Courant,* "stated on Tuesday that he had come one hundred miles on purpose to see them. . . . The most frequent inquiry in our streets is 'which is the road to the jail?' "

Not only in Hartford, but all over the North, people were talking about the *Amistad* captives. Engravings of Nathaniel Jocelyn's portrait of Cinque were being hawked in the streets, and someone had made a gigantic painting of the mutiny— one hundred and thirty-five feet of canvas—and was exhibiting it from town to town. Engravings of this work, which showed Cinque in the act of murdering the cook, were sold as souvenirs. Only ten days after the capture, a "new nautical melodrama" entitled *The Black Schooner, or the Pirate Slaver Amistad* opened at the Bowery Theatre in New York. The principal parts were "Zambra Cinques, Chief of the Muti-

[37

neers," "Lazarillo, Overseer of the Slaves," and "Inez." Unfortunately, the text of this work has disappeared, and we are left to wonder whether "Zambra Cinques" was hero or villain and what "Inez" did to enliven the plot further. The large cast included walk-on parts for all the slaves and all the officers and crew of the *Washington*. *The Black Schooner* took in $1650 the first week (boxes, 75 cents; pit, 37½ cents; gallery, 25 cents), and played to packed houses throughout the autumn of 1839 at various New York theaters—the Park, the National, and Niblo's, as well as at the Bowery.

Even advertisers seized upon the case as an attention-getter: the manufacturers of American Hygiene Pills and Tomato Pills, charging a rival with having stolen their formula, underscored the point with a picture of a schooner and the headline, "PIRATES! The long low black schooner comes again. . . ."

Black people straight from Africa had never been numerous in the North. In New York, the right to trade in slaves or to bring them into the state had been abolished in 1779; in Connecticut, in 1784. The 1830 census had shown twenty-five old slaves still remaining in Connecticut. When these died, the institution would be extinct there. There were several hundred free Negroes in the state, but most of them were not very black and they spoke English like any New Englander. Certainly they seemed a far cry from the "Amistads"—as the African captives came to be called—who were black as coal and whose talk was as mysterious as the twittering of birds in the trees. As for the continent they came from, the average American thought of it vaguely, if he thought of it at all, as a hot, disease-ridden place whose inhabitants were pagan, black, and scarcely human. The arrival of a considerable group of real Africans had at first excited little more than curiosity among the general public; but it had now become apparent that what had at first looked like a side show was a grave matter of conscience, of state, and of history. The press made an effort to appear knowledgeable and to offer its subscribers some background information, but the information tended to vary according to whether the paper favored the Africans or the Spaniards.

The New York *Express*, which sided with Ruiz and Montes, wrote, "Cinque is a Congo. Of these there are several tribes known to slave dealers. Their general character is lazy, mischievous, and apt to run away; lively in their amusements, as music, dancing, etc.; much given to lying, thievery, and all roguery." An *Express* editorial added, "The property will be preciously poor property for the Abolitionists here, as they who have seen these poor fellows represent them to be in appearance hardly above the apes and monkeys of their own Africa, and the language they jabber is incomprehensible here." But, according to the New London *Gazette*, "The tribe to which they belong is one of the noblest in Africa. The more we learn of the man's [Cinque's] character . . . the more are we impressed with a sense of his possessing the true elements of heroism." The New Haven *Herald* adopted a scolding tone: "It will be remarked as a singular fact that this body of 'oppressed humanity', who did not hesitate to spill the blood of others to free themselves from slavery, evinced their attachment to their master and owner by sparing his life and giving him their especial protection. There is evidence in this that they had a kind master and protector and that their social condition could not have been improved. What would have been their condition in Africa had they succeeded in getting there?" Said the Long Island *Star* sarcastically, "On the whole they are the lions of the day and will probably eat many good dinners before they return. If they are not treated with free boxes at the theatres, they may at least expect good pews at the Churches and be properly amalgamated with the audience. We understand the poor fellows are all at Hartford and treated with the utmost kindness. They will undergo an examination and probably will be sent to Havana. Any other course would be repugnant to natural law, and involve us in a controversy with the Government of Spain."

In our day practically all federal cases start out in the district courts. But in 1839 criminal cases such as one involving piracy and murder went directly to the Circuit Court, while such matters as salvage and property claims were handled by the District Court. It was therefore necessary for the *Amistad* case to be heard in both courts. It went first to the United States Circuit Court in Hartford, on the morning of September 19, 1839. The presiding judge was a Supreme Court Justice, Smith Thompson.

Mr. Holabird, on behalf of the United States government, was the first to speak. He straightway asked the judge to issue a mandate, placing the matter in the hands of the Executive. In this way it would be up to the President to decide whether the captives ought to be delivered up to Spain or returned to Africa. He then argued at great length in favor of delivering them to Spain.

Mr. Seth Staples, for the prisoners, asked for a writ of habeas corpus so that at least the children, who were not charged with piracy, might be released. The judge granted the writ and said that when it should be returned next day he would decide whether to act upon it or whether the children would have to be detained as property.

"But," said Mr. Roger Baldwin, "how came these Negroes to be slaves or property? Were they born owing allegiance to the Spanish Government? Not at all. They are natives of Africa. How came they so far subject to the Spanish laws as to be judged by them? How is it, when these persons come before our court asserting their liberty, that they are to be judged by Spanish laws? Have these children ever been domiciled in Spain? They were torn from their parents in Africa; forcibly landed in the island of Cuba, late at night, and cruelly sold to these men."

Late at night! Baldwin had scored a point. In New England, the idea of keeping children up late at night was almost as outrageous as enslaving them. He went on to speak of a case in which two hundred white Christian captives had mutinied aboard an Algerian ship in the Mediterranean and had succeeded in bringing it to Malta, where the Knights of Malta immediately set them free and helped them to return to their homes in eastern Europe. The sultan of Turkey had threatened war and then demanded compensation, but in the end had done nothing. Baldwin pointed out that if the *Amistad* Africans had been white Christians and Ruiz and Montes had been Algerians, the question before the court that morning would have been considered quite a different one.

Ignoring this argument, District Attorney Holabird insisted that the Africans were foreign property and cited Article 9 of the Treaty of 1795. That morning he had written to the Secretary of State, "I should regret extremely if the rascally blacks should fall into the hands of the abolitionists, with whom Hartford is filled."

Captain Henry Green testified that he had seen the Africans bringing trunks to the shore. The trunks, he said, had rattled and had looked heavy to lift. Later, when opened, they were empty. "Some person or persons are supposed to have the money but where is a secret," reported the newspapers. Later, Lieutenant Meade sued Lewis Tappan for having suggested publicly that Meade knew where the doubloons were.

Mr. Baldwin criticized the conduct of Lieutenant Gedney. "Do our treaties impose upon our navy and judicial officers the duty of being slave-catchers for foreign slave-holders?" He was an eloquent speaker, and went on in this vein for two and a half hours.

On the fourth day Judge Thompson gave his opinion that the Circuit Court had no jurisdiction over the charges of murder and mutiny. The alleged crimes had been committed on a Spanish ship in Spanish waters, and American laws against piracy covered only our territorial waters and American ships on the high seas. As for the property claims, they must be decided in District Court. He denied the motion of the defense to have either all the prisoners or the children alone discharged under the writ of habeas corpus for the reason that the property claims were yet to be decided. In view of certain precedents set by American courts in other cases, he could not rule that the United States opposed the right of property in human beings. In those cases, he said, "the courts did not say you can not set up the right of property in persons; but they have said to the claimants, *you must show your title*. The burthen of proof rests on you. We are not in a position to be influenced . . . by any private feeling we may have. We are called upon to administer a system of laws, equally applicable in a State where slavery is not, and where it is, tolerated. My feelings personally are as abhorrent to the right of slavery as perhaps those of any man who has appeared in this cause. . . . We do not decide, in disallowing the habeas corpus, that these parties are not entitled to their freedom, but only that it is in a regular way for decision, in another tribunal, from whose decision an appeal may be taken to this court, and if desired, to the Supreme Court of the United States."

As soon as Judge Thompson adjourned the Circuit Court, Judge Andrew Judson immediately convened the District Court in the same courtroom. Having heard the arguments of the various lawyers, Judson gave it as his opinion that the question of whether the Africans should be returned to the Spanish claimants as property needed more investigation. He also made it clear that neither the *Washington* officers nor Captain Green could expect to sell the Negroes for salvage claims, slave trading being illegal in both Connecticut and New York. The judge was willing to release the prisoners on bail, but in that case, he said, there would have to be an appraisal of their value on the Cuban slave market. Their counsel would not hear of such a thing and therefore all the captives were returned to jail. Judge Judson directed the United States Marshal, Mr. Wilcox, to find some other place than the New Haven county jail in which to detain them, for they were no longer to be held as criminals. The District Court then adjourned, setting the third Tuesday of November for further hearing of the case.

4

THE PRISONERS' STORY

While the Hartford trials were going on, Forsyth wrote again to Calderón, asking whether he had any documents to support the Spanish side of the case, other than the *Amistad*'s papers. Calderón did not answer until ten days later. By that time he must have known what had happened at Hartford, but all he said was that his tour of duty in Washington was up, and his replacement, Caballero Pedro Alcántara Argaiz, had arrived. "The case belongs to Señor Argaiz," he told Forsyth in the best bureaucratic tradition. He added that he had no other documents to offer other than the *Amistad*'s papers, "of the lawfulness of which there appears to be no reason for doubt."

On October 3 the Caballero de Argaiz wrote his first letter on the subject of the *Amistad:* "The undersigned, envoy extraordinary and minister plenipotentiary of Her Catholic Majesty, has the honor of commencing his official correspondence with you, sir, by soliciting an act of justice. . . ." Argaiz's style was more flamboyant than his predecessor's; he would have ample opportunity to practice it. In this letter he ignored the Hartford proceedings and confined himself to quoting a letter from the Spanish vice-consul at Boston, who said that it seemed strange to him that the *Amistad* and her cargo had not yet been turned back into Spanish hands. Argaiz "doubts not" that Forsyth will take care of the matter without delay.

Forsyth, whose position was becoming more and more embarrassing, did not answer this letter for several weeks, though he probably had private talks with Señor Argaiz that kept that gentleman from writing again. Meanwhile, the President had asked the Attorney General, Felix Grundy, of Tennessee, for an opinion of the case. Grundy prepared a very long one, the gist of which was that the United States had no business to question the papers of the *Amistad,* for that road would lead to the untenable position of passing judgment on an Anglo-Spanish treaty and on certain internal laws of Spain. American law could not affect Spanish law, he said. Furthermore, the Negroes were property, like any other cargo, and should be handed over to whoever could prove right of ownership. As a precedent for his arguments, Grundy cited the case of the *Antelope,* one of the most vexing matters that had ever come before the young republic's Supreme Court. It had filled volumes of legal records from 1820 to 1827, in which year it was finally settled.*

Grundy went on to consider whether or not the mutiny of the Africans came under the heading of piracy. His answer was that it did not—because pirates sail under no flag and are therefore subject to punishment by any nation that apprehends them, whereas the *Amistad* was a Spanish ship and the mutiny had occurred in Spanish waters against Spanish subjects. Its mutineers, therefore, must go before a Spanish tri-

* See Appendix II.

bunal. Lastly, he dealt with the problem of what should be done with the vessel and its cargo, "the negroes being part of the latter." It was true, of course, that an act of Congress of 1818 prohibited the import of slaves into the United States and required that those illegally imported should be returned to Africa. But this act was not applicable in this case, he said, because the *Amistad* had not come to the United States with a view to selling slaves. However, he argued, the case clearly fell under the ninth article of the Treaty of 1795, concerning ships rescued from pirates or robbers; and whether or not the rescue took place on the seas made no difference —"the vessel and cargo should be restored entire, as far as practicable."

Grundy, therefore, recommended that since the owners of the vessel (the heirs of the murdered captain) were not in the United States, the Spanish minister should take custody of vessel and cargo. And, he concluded, with a sudden concern for the rights of the Africans, "these negroes deny that they are slaves; if they should be delivered to the claimants [Ruiz and Montes] no opportunity may be afforded for the assertion of their right to freedom. For these reasons, it seems to me that a delivery to the Spanish minister is the only safe course for this Government to pursue."

President Van Buren allowed Grundy's opinion to be conveyed privately to Señor Argaiz, who was told that it was that of "a learned lawyer," and had been adopted by the cabinet. Van Buren, Forsyth, and Grundy must have deplored the judgment of cautious Mr. Holabird in allowing the case ever to get into the courts; for to get it out of them now involved very tangled red tape indeed. It was a difficult matter to explain to Señor Argaiz, who came from a country where there was no curb on the executive power. Nobody questioned what the Queen or her ministers decided, and it was incomprehensible to Argaiz that the wishes of the President should be thwarted by an obscure judge, some busybody private citizens, and a gang of mutinous blacks.

After the Hartford trials Cinque was relieved of his irons, in accordance with Judge Judson's order that the Africans should no longer be treated as criminals. On the journey back to New Haven, he was allowed to sit beside the driver of the stage. A New Haven *Herald* reporter wrote that he was "passing the City Hotel when the stage stopped there and the driver having occasion to alight, placed the reins in the hands of Jingua [Cinque]. He seemed delighted at the confidence reposed in him and we presume for the moment felt as free as his situation seemed to indicate."

Ensconced once more in the New Haven county jail, the whole group settled down to study English and theology. Students from the Yale Divinity School taught them for two to five hours a day, showing them pictures of objects, then pronouncing the English words for them, and then writing the words down. The pupils seemed interested and sometimes complained of too short hours. They grew fond of some of the teachers, clinging to their hands, and offering them their dinner. But when one of the clergymen, Dr. Gallaudet,* asked them if they thought murder was punishable by God, they became suddenly very apprehensive. Cinque ("who can scowl as deep as any one") warned his companions that Gallaudet might be an agent of the Spaniards, sent to trick them into a confession. But John Ferry, the interpreter, convinced them that Gallaudet had meant no harm, and they all came up to shake hands.

They had now been supplied with checked cotton shirts,

* Gallaudet was the founder of the first free school for the deaf and dumb in America.

cotton and wool trousers, wool socks, and thick shoes. The frosty New England autumn had set in, and their rooms were somewhat overheated by a stove. Visitors noted an offensive stench, due (according to what paper you read) either to the prisoners' natural uncleanliness or to the fact that some of them suffered from bowel complaints and there were no sanitary facilities other than chamber pots, which were in the same rooms where they slept and ate. Joshua Leavitt wrote to the newspapers, saying that the jail quarters were not clean enough; the prisoners had no change of shirts; and, because they had no coats, could not go out. A lady had given Cinque a frock coat and a clean shirt, but the jailer had taken them away. Worse still, the three little girls slept in one bed with the little boy in a room accessible to the men. Someone else commented that the jailer "had little or no sympathy with the people committed to his charge and was jealous of every visitor who he suspects is unlike himself. . . . He was thoroughly uncivil."

These complaints brought about a visit to the jail by seven New Haven selectmen. Their verdict was that the Africans were comfortable, had ample clothing, that their rooms were nicely warmed, and that they were contented and happy. Dr. Charles Hooker, the physician in charge, added that the Africans seemed to find clothing burdensome and would not wear what they had, for which the jailer could not be blamed. An editorial in one of the New Haven newspapers commented sternly, "There are white men in the prison not so comfortably clad as the Africans. Would it not be well to show a little sympathy for them?"

So much had been written about the Africans that the public was beginning to think of them as individuals, not as a characterless crowd. One newspaper apologized for having called Ko-no-ma a cannibal. "The only reason for this appellation is that his teeth, according to our notions, are not very well-arranged, and a degree of emaciation leaving him but a skeleton, made him in face a frightful object." All the captives (their teachers announced with relief) "professed abhorrence of eating the flesh of humans."

Bur-na, the young man who had not gone to Hartford because he was too ill, recovered rapidly. He was dejected and worried while his companions were away. One of his teachers noted that "he manifests much feeling when reference is made to his companions who have died. It has been commonly estimated that thirteen of the number have died since they left Havana; but Bur-na asserts, positively, that the number is fourteen. He places three cents together to represent those who have died in this town, another for the one buried at New London, ten for those who died on the water; and then makes a pile of twenty-three for those who died while they were bound. Whether the latter number comprises those only who died at Havana, or all since their leaving Africa and previous to their departure from Havana could not be determined.

"Very incorrect reports are given in some newspapers in regard to the appearance and character of these captives. Gentlemen, however, who have been accustomed to see Africans in their native country, in the West Indies, and in our southern states, affirm that they have never seen a better collection of blacks. They generally have not the broad flat noses, the thick lips and the low foreheads that characterize most Africans, and they seem to be a superior variety of people to the blacks commonly seen in this country. They appear to disadvantage from the circumstances that they have little means of communication with those round them except by signs, and that more than one third of their number were much emaciated and enfeebled by disease when they came to this town; but they are by no means deficient in intellectual qualities or in sensibility, as has been represented in some newspapers.

"One of them had a painful decayed tooth, which required extraction. His companions earnestly encouraged him to submit to the operation, and one of them, Kim-bo, stood behind to hold his head; but during the operation he turned his own head aside, and afterwards gave the physician to understand that he could never bear to witness such operations, and that when the Captain of the schooner was killed, he could not see it done, but looked another way."

When two of their number died, the Yale missionaries took the occasion for sermons on immortality. "The soul of Ka-pe-ri is alive," one of the clergymen told them. "It will never die. Our souls will never die. They will live after our bodies are dead and cold. The Bible tells us how our souls may go to the good place. You must learn to read the Bible. Pray to God, become good, and then when your bodies die, God will take your souls to the good place and make you happy forever."

According to observers, the Africans heard this with serious attention and seemed anxious to learn to read the Bible—"this is the great desire of their hearts." However, they did not like the stillness that prevailed at Christian funerals, and accounted for it "only on the grounds of insensibility." At the funeral that they themselves conducted for the first prisoner to die in New Haven, Tu-a, they all wept and moaned loudly. Tu-a and three others who died during the month of September were buried in a corner of the New Haven burying ground.

For the most part, the Africans were eager and cooperative students, anxious to assent to whatever their teachers wished. However, one of them, Gil-a-ba-ru, insisted that he did not know what becomes of the good or the bad when they die, for he had never been dead. Bur-na, one of the star pupils, begged one of the clergymen to accompany them back to Africa.

"But should I go with you, what good could I do you?" the teacher asked.

"Teach us," Bur-na replied.

"But if I go I must teach you truth. The Bible says that a man must have but *one* wife. Will you put away *all* but *one?*"

They all said they would.

Dr. Gibbs was still spending his spare time on the New York docks, and at last, early in October, he happened on a real Mende-speaker. He was a seaman on board the British warship *Buzzard,* which had been on slave-ship patrol and had put into New York harbor for supplies. The seaman, James Covey, was about twenty years old. Like John Ferry, he had been rescued from a slaver by the British and taken to Freetown, where he had been brought up in a family of liberated blacks. His name had been changed, he said, from Kaw-wa-li ("War-road") to James by an Anglican clergyman. His native tongue was Mende, though he remembered it imperfectly and now spoke and thought in English, or rather in the English dialect of Freetown, Kreo.

When Covey appeared in the New Haven jail and greeted the prisoners in Mende, there were whoops of joy. "They leaped, shouted, and clapped their hands," said an observer. At last they could tell their side of the story.

They began by explaining that they belonged to six different tribes. All came from that part of West Africa of which the largest tribe is the Mende. With a couple of exceptions, they were not related to one another, and had met for the first time at the "slave factory" of Pedro Blanco, a notorious slave trader on the island of Lomboko, south of Freetown.

[51

Cinque had been kidnapped by members of another tribe near his village, which, he said, was ten days' march from Lomboko. Kidnapping was the usual recourse of slave traders. Some of the other Africans said that they had been taken in war or had been sold by their own tribes to another, either because of debt or because of what was genteelly described in New England as crim. con. (adultery). After months or in some cases years of slavery in alien tribes, they had been taken down to Lomboko and sold to Pedro Blanco.

At Lomboko Pedro Blanco sold them to the master of a Portuguese slave ship. When the master had accumulated six or seven hundred slaves, he stowed them into his ship's hold and chained them two-and-two in a half-lying position. Soon after this slaver had put to sea, she was chased by a British cruiser, and so put back into Lomboko and landed the slaves. The British had then seized the ship and taken her to Freetown. After some time the slaves were put aboard another Portuguese ship, the *Teçora*, and taken to the Caribbean by way of the Middle Passage. Quarters on the *Teçora* were even worse than on the previous slaver. The slaves were naked, were fed bad food, and were flogged for not eating. Vinegar and gunpowder were rubbed into their wounds. Many died at sea. At length they reached a harbor near Havana and were landed under cover of night. The next night, in chains, they walked through the streets of Havana to a barracoon, an oblong, roofless enclosure, something like a pen for cattle. Purchasers came daily to look them over, and after ten days Pedro Montes came and bought the children and José Ruiz bought forty-nine adults. From the barracoon they were taken (again at night) to the *Amistad*, lying in the harbor.

Conditions were less horrifying aboard the *Amistad* than they had been on the *Teçora*, though scarcely pleasant. The slaves were chained below decks by means of iron collars, each connected to his neighbor, the whole string of collars being secured by one chain to the wall. They were brought on deck to eat. A single plantain, some bread, and a cup of water constituted a day's rations. One of them who tried to take water from a cask was severely flogged by the captain. When they asked the cook, a mulatto slave, for more food, the answer was that they soon would need none at all—for when they arrived at Príncipe, he told them, they would have their throats cut and be chopped in pieces and salted down as meat for the Spaniards. He pointed to some barrels of beef, then to an empty barrel, and "by talking with his fingers" (as the Africans said) made them understand what lay in store.

On the third day out, when the slaves went on deck to eat, Cinque found a nail, which he secreted under his arm. Then, back in the hold, they held a council. One of them, Kin-na (after he had learned some English), described it this way: "We feel bad, and we ask Cinque what to do. Cinque say, 'Me think and by and by I tell you.' Cinque then said, 'If we do nothing, we be killed. We may as well die in trying to be free as to be killed and eaten.'"

With the aid of the nail, Cinque managed to break the chain that fastened them all to the wall. Then they separated the chains that bound them together. All, except the children, armed themselves with cane-knives, which they found in the hold, and stole out upon the deck. There was rain and fog and they were able to steal up on the cook and on the captain, who was at the wheel, before either knew what was happening. Cinque killed the cook with a single blow. The captain fought desperately, killing one African and wounding two others before he himself was killed. The two white sailors went over the side. "They could not catch land," said Kin-na, "they must have swum to the bottom of the sea." However, it turned out later that they had launched the stern boat and eventually reached Havana with tidings of the mutiny.

Cinque now took command, and everyone at once helped himself to plenty to eat and drink. Meantime Ruiz and Montes, who had fled to the hold, were dragged out and put in irons. When they cried and begged not to be chained (according to Kin-na), Cinque said, "You say fetters good for Negro; if good for Negro, good for Spanish man, too; you try them two days and see how they feel." The Spaniards asked for water and each received one small cupful, just as had been given the Africans. Cinque told them, "You say little water enough for nigger; if little water do for him, a little do for you, too." Cinque, through the interpreter, James Covey, said that the Spaniards cried a great deal, and that he had felt sorry for them. He had only meant to let them see how it was to be treated like the poor slaves. After two days he took their irons off, and then (said Cinque) gave them plenty of water and food and treated them very well. Kin-na stated that when water fell short, Cinque would not drink any or allow any of the rest to drink, but dealt out a little to each of the children and the same quantity to the two Spaniards.

Ruiz and Montes composed a letter and told Cinque to hail the next vessel he saw, give the letter to the master, and he would surely take them to Sierra Leone. Cinque said, "Very well," and took the letter. But to his companions he said, "We have no letter in Mende. I don't know what is in the letter— there may be death in it. So we will take some iron and a string, bind them about the letter, and send it to the bottom of the sea."

On another occasion, while they were on the high seas, Cinque asked Montes to throw out the anchor. Montes replied that the water was too deep. Cinque dived as deep as he could, found no bottom, and decided that, for once, Montes was telling the truth.

After that, the Africans' story of the wanderings of the *Amistad* was essentially the same as that told by Ruiz and Montes. Cinque knew that Montes was trying to cheat him by sailing in the wrong direction, but because of "sympathy" (and also, no doubt, because Montes knew how to control the ship) forebore to kill him.

During the third week in October, when the public was beginning to weary of the *Amistad* case, a new and dramatic development brought it back into the headlines. A Spanish-language New York newspaper was first with the news: "IN WHAT COUNTRY DO WE LIVE?" demanded an indignant headline.

> Are we, peradventure, in some land inhabited by savages —are we under the despotic sway of the Grand Sultan? . . . No, sir; we are in a republic where we are told there are laws—where we are told the rights of man are sacred —where we are told property is protected—where they speak of affording hospitality and an asylum to the stranger—where they say we are *all* free—where the constitution of the land says so—where the slavery of the negro is recognized—where the very Congress has forbidden the reading within that body of petitions in favor of the slaves—where the government has refused to recognize the independence of Santo Domingo to avoid the reception of a black ambassador at Washington. . . .

What was the cause of all this fulmination? Two of the Africans, Fon-ne and Kim-bo, had brought charges of assault, kidnapping, and false imprisonment against Ruiz and Montes, and both Spaniards had been clapped into prison.

[55

5

"IT IS A NATIONAL MATTER"

It was the lawyers of the *Amistad* committee, of course, who had arranged this surprise move, filing the affidavits in New York City, where both Ruiz and Montes were staying. Bail was set at one thousand dollars each, but when it was later reduced to a nominal sum, friends of Montes paid his. He immediately jumped it and departed for Cuba. Ruiz refused bail and stayed in prison, with the idea of stirring up public sympathy for his case. "It is a national matter," said he. The prison was the Tombs, then a new building and not the horror it later became. Ruiz had a pleasantly furnished cell and was allowed out for walks and to dine with friends. Still, he was in jail, and even those with moderate sympathy toward the Africans thought the abolitionists had gone too far.

"This conduct of our misguided zealots," said the New York *Courier & Enquirer*, "is not merely censurable on the score of frivolity and wantonness of thus making sport of the law and perverting the powers of courts of justice to factious and fanatical ends; but it is highly unpatriotic, because it tends directly to involve the whole United States in hostilities with the Government of Spain, with which we are now on the best terms."

The New Haven *Register* was even more severe:

> The papers . . . speak indignantly of this arrest of Montes and Ruiz and their incarceration in a jail, at the pretended suit of two of these savages; a suit which they know no more about than the man in the moon, but which has been got up in their names by certain abolitionists. . . . After the fatigues and hardships which they [Montes and Ruiz] endured on their late cruise in the Atlantic, and the personal violence and abuse they received from Cinquez and his fellows, to be thus shamefully dealt with . . . is abominably wicked. The negroes can be made to say anything that their pseudo friends require, having not the least idea of accountability or conscience. They have been petted by many of the visitors to the jail until they have become quite obstinate and unmanageable. . . . We would as soon think of going to a henroost or a hog sty—as far as procuring correct statement depends—as to these negroes."

The Spanish minister immediately fired off a furious ten-thousand-word letter to Mr. Forsyth. First, he pointed out that it would be possible to throw the case out of court through a legal loophole: Ruiz had been named in the arrest order as "Pipi," whereas Ruiz's name was José, or, in the diminutive, "Pepe." "Thus it appears that a Pepe has been imprisoned instead of a Pipi, which I believe the law does not permit." Then Argaiz went on to say that, in any event, the New York court had no jurisdiction over Spaniards in connection with alleged crimes committed in Cuba, and that the President ought to order their immediate release. He added that he would like to have the matter settled in time to send word to Spain by a packet that would be sailing on the first of November. He was anxious to calm "the disquiet . . . in the mind of Her Majesty." (Queen Isabella II of Spain was then eleven years old. If she concerned herself at all with affairs of state, it is more likely that her mind was disquieted by the bloody civil war that had been raging all about her ever since her accession to the throne at the age of five.)

Secretary Forsyth replied within forty-eight hours, but had not much to say that would reassure the Queen. He noted, somewhat inaccurately, that the courts of our country were open to all without distinction, and pointed out that our Constitution and laws secure the judicial power against all interference on the part of the Executive. However, he added, the State Department had instructed the United States District Attorney for New York to get in touch with Messrs. Montes and Ruiz and offer them any services possible.

In his next letter Argaiz mentions having had a long conversation with the New York District Attorney which "left him delighted with [his] affability and courtesy . . . although he did not have the happiness to remain satisfied as to the principal matter." He also refers to certain private conferences with Mr. Forsyth, but these have remained off the record and we will never know what Forsyth said to mollify him. Argaiz notes with pleasure that Forsyth has made no attempt to argue with the Spanish point of view, but has only endeavored to explain the mysteries of the American judicial system. Separation of power was gibberish to Argaiz.

> As the incompetence of the courts of the United States with regard to this matter is so clearly demonstrated, is there no power in the Federal Government to declare it so? . . . Her Catholic Majesty's envoy extraordinary and minister plenipotentiary . . . asks the Secretary of State whether or

not he possesses sufficient authority and force to carry into fulfillment the Treaty of 1795. If he has not, then there can be no treaty binding on the other party.

This threat must have precipitated further off-the-record conferences between Her Catholic Majesty's envoy and Mr. Forsyth, for there were no more letters for several weeks.

The District Court sat again on October 19 to consider the matter of the *Amistad*'s place of seizure. According to law, if the *Amistad* had been within the territorial waters of New York when she was taken by the *Washington*, the case belonged to the New York District Court. If she had been on the high seas, the case belonged in the District Court of Connecticut, the state where she had been brought into port. It was now established that when the *Washington* took charge of her, she had been anchored about a mile from a shore without inlets or bays. On such a shoreline, according to the laws of admiralty, "high seas" extend to the low-water mark. Judge Judson ruled, therefore, that the case was properly in the District Court of Connecticut rather than in that of New York. He also set a date in November for the hearing of some new evidence that had come to his attention. He had had a letter from the head of the British Antislavery Commission in Havana, Dr. Robert Madden, who had read of the case and was offering to come to Connecticut and give testimony concerning the condition of Cuban blacks. Madden's job in Havana was a frustrating one; most of the time he could do nothing but watch the breaking of laws that he was being paid to see enforced. The *Amistad* case gave him a chance, at last, to make himself useful, and he made the most of it.

Robert Madden was born in Ireland in 1798 and died there

eighty-eight years later. Most of the years between were spent in such diverse places as the Near East, West Africa, the Caribbean, and Australia, usually in pursuit of his greatest interest, ridding the world of slavery. While employed at the thankless task of watching the Spanish in Cuba violate their treaty with England, he gave vent to his outrage in reams of antislavery verse—heartfelt, if not first class. For example:

> We are not always scourging—by the way,
> Tuesday in common is our flogging day.
> At other times we only use the whip
> To stir the drones and make the young ones skip.
> Then as to food, you may be sure we give
> Enough to let the wretched creatures live.
> The diet's somewhat slender, there's no doubt
> It would not do to let them grow too stout.

He had also recently published, in Boston, a pamphlet, "Regarding the Slave Trade in Cuba." It was written in the form of a letter to the Reverend William Ellery Channing, a Boston cleric who opposed slavery but opposed abolitionism as well—believing, he said, that God would indicate when the time was ripe for abolishing slavery. ("If a good work cannot be carried on by the calm, self-controlled benevolent spirit of Christianity," he said, "then the time for doing it has not come.")

Madden's pamphlet had achieved a wide circulation in the United States shortly before the *Amistad* incident, and even provoked an anonymous rebuttal "By a Calm Observer." Using language that "Calm Observer" found intemperate, Madden denounced the Cuban authorities for winking at the slave trade in return for from ten to fifteen dollars per illegally imported slave. He also charged that because there was a great amount of American capital in Cuba, dependent on plentiful slave labor, the United States Consul at Havana, Nicholas P. Trist, was conniving to "give a new impetus to the illegal traffic in human beings" and to "render it impossible" for the British to suppress the traffic. Trist (said Madden) knew that American ships visited the slave coast under Portuguese colors; he knew also that slavers of Portuguese and other nationalities used American ships for their stores. He condoned these things and was ready to give the American captains falsified documents when they needed them. He abetted the shipping of slaves from Havana to Texas (then an independent republic) as "free indentured labor."

According to Madden, Consul Trist made no bones about his slaveholding beliefs and called abolitionists "self-seekers, deceivers, theatrical exhibitors, fanatics, and impostors," for whom he felt nothing but "disgust and indignation." Madden quotes him as having said in a letter, "I now entertain a deliberate and oft-revolved doubt whether considered merely in itself, the slave-trade be not a positive benefit to its supposed victims. Were the trade open and regulated in the way that emigrant vessels are, I should entertain no doubt on the subject."

If these were his sentiments, Trist must have been happy in his Havana post. Despite the treaty expressly forbidding the slave trade and despite the continual protests of Dr. Madden's Antislavery Commission, more than twenty-five thousand slaves had been brought into Cuba from Africa in the past three years. Under the treaty British cruisers were permitted to patrol Spanish waters for slave ships. Whenever they caught one, they handed the slaves over to the Spanish colonial authorities with the understanding that they were to be treated as free, and "instructed in the Christian religion and taught some trade by which they were enabled to earn their bread."

"It is a lamentable fact," wrote Madden in his pamphlet, "that from the year 1820 to 1830, of some 14 or 15 thousand of these unfortunate negroes called *emancipados* delivered over to the Spanish authorities in Cuba, *one* individual only has obtained freedom." The government "apprenticed" them for periods of five, seven, or ten years. They were thus worse off than slaves, for their masters had no lifetime investment to protect. And, to get back to Trist (who was never far from Madden's thoughts), he was said to have in his household an *emancipada* whom he sent out to peddle fruit in the streets and whose earnings he kept for himself.

Nicholas Trist was married to Virginia Randolph, a granddaughter of Thomas Jefferson, and as a very young man had studied law under the great man himself. After serving as Andrew Jackson's private secretary, he had taken the Havana post in 1834. The salary was two thousand dollars a year and the climate was considered very dangerous for persons unaccustomed to the tropics; Mrs. Trist and her children were seldom with him. Nevertheless, the position held certain attractions. The American consul's notary fees alone came to more than his salary. Trist further supplemented this income through investments he made for American businessmen. By 1839 he had paid off his debts, which had been considerable, owned a dairy farm, and was sending his children to school in France. He had also made a great many enemies, and in the summer of the same year a group of Americans in Cuba, who were joined enthusiastically by nearly two hundred sea captains, petitioned Congress for his removal, charging him with inefficiency, with failing to uphold American interests, and with abetting the slave trade. Congress referred the petition to its Committee on Commerce. After months of deliberation, the committee announced that it could find no case against him. Since no one had come openly to his defense, rumor had it that no less a person than Andrew Jackson had intervened behind the scenes. He was replaced as consul in 1841, but remained profitably occupied in Cuba until the Polk administration, four years later, at which time he was sent to Mexico and earned a respectable niche for himself in history by helping to negotiate the Treaty of Guadelupe-Hidalgo.

Dr. Madden, in his pamphlet and in the testimony he gave before Judge Judson, called Trist "a political pygmy," "arrogant," "rude," "incapable," "intractable," "injudicious," "overbearing," "dishonest," "vain," "a third-rate dangler on official life," and "this official chimpanzee." In his zeal to get rid of him, Madden either ignored or did not understand the nuances of Anglo-American relations in the Caribbean. The Americans were ever suspicious of England's territorial ambitions there. As everyone knew, the Spanish Empire was gradually but steadily falling apart. Someday, Cuba would go. When it went, no American statesman, whether Northerner or Southerner, wanted to see it fall into the hands of the not-so-long-ago enemy. And there were many who feared that the British Antislavery Commission in Havana was gathering evidence against Spain regarding the broken treaty, evidence that would someday be used as an excuse for seizing the island.

The abolitionists were so intent upon outlawing slavery that most of them looked to England as an example to be emulated, not as a possible wolf in sheep's clothing. Lewis Tappan, in his political unworldliness, thought England should make a treaty with Texas similar to the one with Spain, making Texas a substantial loan or grant in return for abolishing slavery. "My plan is for the British nation to buy up Texas," he wrote to *The Emancipator*. "Let her lavish money upon the undertaking for she can never take a step so directly tending to the extinction of slavery. . . . What I mean by buying is that she shall, in some way, and at all cost, make it most obviously the interest of Texas to abolish slavery."

Dr. Madden arrived in New York in the middle of November 1839, and after a visit to the Africans in the New Haven county jail, went to Hartford to give his deposition. He covered substantially the same points as he had made in his pamphlet, adding evidence to show that Ruiz had not bought the slaves for his own use but in behalf of an uncle, who had planned to resell them in Puerto Príncipe. He also told the court that he had carefully observed the Africans in New Haven and that they were without question recently from Africa and knew nothing of Cuba or the Spanish language.

Having given his testimony, Madden went to Washington, where he gave the British minister, Henry S. Fox, a full account of the case, and tried without success to see President Van Buren. He then departed for London, where he had an audience with Queen Victoria on the subject of the *Amistad*. Madden's efforts led to a note from Mr. Fox to Mr. Forsyth, pointing out in detail the lawlessness of the Cuban authorities and adding that Her Britannic Majesty took a personal interest in the just settlement of the case. Forsyth's reply was not nearly so friendly as his replies to the Spanish minister, for he shared the prevailing American suspicion of British purposes in the Caribbean. In the coldest diplomatic style, he advised Fox to mind his own business.

Fortunately for the Africans, they had another friend in high places, one who could do more for them than the Queen of England. This friend was John Quincy Adams, who continued to follow their case with keen interest. He noted in his diary all the details of the Hartford trial and said he had been studying the matter at length—"an enormous consumption of time only to perplex myself with a multitude of questions upon which I cannot yet make up opinions for which I am willing to be responsible." Parts of his letter to William Jay on the subject had been published in the papers, presumably with his permission, thus giving great prestige to the African cause and adding, if this were possible, to his bad reputation in the South.

"Gracious heavens, my dear Sir, your mind is diseased on the subject of slavery," a Virginia lady wrote to him. "Pray what had you to do with the captured ship? . . . You are great in everything else, but here you show your weakness. Your name will descend to the latest posterity with this blot on it: Mr. Adams loves the negroes too much unconstitutionally." A less restrained person in North Carolina sent him an engraved portrait of himself with a bullet hole through the forehead and the inscription "to stop the music of John Quincy Adams." The old man took grim pleasure in showing this letter and the picture in the House.

In 1839 Adams was in his eighth year in Congress. To quote Emerson, he was "a man of audacious independence that always kept the public curiosity alive in regard to what he might do. . . . A bruiser . . . who cannot live on slops but must have sulphuric acid in his tea." All his life he had had these characteristics, and as he grew older they became more pronounced. He did what he thought best for the country, little caring what people said. He was avowedly opposed to slavery, but disappointed the abolitionists by refusing to join them. He thought most of them were fanatics who did more harm to their cause than good, and he feared lest their agitation should disrupt the Union. Yet for the last three years in Congress he had been fighting the Gag Rule—a Southern resolution that made it illegal to discuss slavery in the House. He fought it not because he wished to discuss slavery in the House, but because such a rule was unconstitutional. In the

South he was massively despised, and even in his own Massachusetts there were many gentlemen of his own class and breeding who refused to speak to him, believing that slavery was the concern of the South alone. His wife and sons constantly urged him to avoid the abolitionists. His constituents in Plymouth, however, were mostly old-fashioned people imbued with the standards of their Revolutionary grandfathers and they approved the old man's uncompromising, dispassionate attitudes and his faith in the Union and the Constitution.

6

ON TRIAL IN NEW HAVEN

The winter of 1839 and 1840 was the coldest and snowiest that New Englanders could remember. As the New Year opened, there were over two feet of snow on the ground, and travel between towns was by sleigh or snowshoe only. Stages filled with passengers had to pass whole nights in the open countryside. A Springfield-Boston train became snowbound in a wood, and twenty-six passengers, including ladies, had to sleep all night in the cars, with the temperature outside at fourteen below. They were rescued next morning by sleighs. There were reports of people going a short distance by foot or on horseback, suddenly sinking beyond their depth, and dying in the effort to extract themselves. Ice prevented ships from entering New York harbor; even as far south as Washington, the Potomac was blocked, and the thermometer stood at several degrees below zero.

Citizens of New Haven were surprised and curious when they saw the United States naval schooner *Grampus* sailing into the harbor. Naval maneuvers were seldom carried out in winter and never in such a time of storm and cold. The young commander of the vessel, Lieutenant Paine, would say only that he was there under secret orders. District Attorney Holabird, who knew what the orders were, kept mum, although he was seething with nervousness. As he was aware, there had been another spate of letters between the Spanish minister and the American Secretary of State. Argaiz's mood had been sulky and threatening. Forsyth, to mollify him, had promised that as soon as the Connecticut court should decide the case against the Africans, they would be sent back to Cuba aboard an American naval vessel. He assured Argaiz that President Van Buren himself had ordered a vessel to stand by at New Haven and had also directed Lieutenants Gedney and Meade to go to Cuba along with the prisoners, in order to contribute testimony at the trial in Havana.

The *Grampus* was one of the smallest ships in the United States Navy. Lieutenant Paine had written to his superiors to point out that it would be impossible to accommodate all the prisoners below decks, and that in the event of a storm those on deck would be in constant danger of being swept overboard. He was told, in a crisp official reply, to treat the passengers, prisoners and all, with all possible attention. Mr. Forsyth, who was apparently confident that the court decision could go no other way than against the Africans, sent Mr. Holabird a warrant, signed by the President, authorizing the United States Marshal to take immediate charge of the prisoners after the trial and clap them into irons aboard the *Grampus*. "If the decision of the court is such as is anticipated," Forsyth wrote, "the order of the President is to be carried into execution, unless an appeal shall actually have been interposed. And if, on the contrary, the decision of the court is different, you are to take out an appeal, and allow things to remain as they are until the appeal shall have been decided."

Holabird noticed that, through an oversight, the warrant named the place of trial as the Circuit Court instead of the District Court. Ever cautious, he sent it back to Washington by fast messenger for correction; but when it was returned, the word "circuit" had merely been crossed out and "district" written in above it. Holabird feared that if the *Amistad* committee should decide to make an issue of the matter, the warrant might be ruled invalid.

On the morning of January 8, the Africans were bundled into coats, mufflers, and boots collected by the *Amistad* committee, and marched across New Haven Green to the courthouse. The lawyers who had defended them in Hartford—Staples, Sedgwick, and Baldwin—were again present, and there were also lawyers to represent the Spanish owners of the *Amistad*, the Spanish Crown, Lieutenant Gedney and the other *Washington* officers, and Captain Henry Green of Sag Harbor. All the seats in the courtroom were taken, and people stayed in them through the lunch hour in order not to lose them. There were many women among the spectators. Yale law classes had been adjourned so that the students could hear this important case.

The defense began by introducing evidence to show that the prisoners were recently from Africa. Dr. Gibbs was called as a linguistic expert. Mr. Holabird, who was representing the Spanish Crown, objected that Gibbs's evidence was worthless because it was based on information obtained from James Covey, the African interpreter. Roger Baldwin argued that a skilled linguist could tell whether or not a person spoke a language with an admixture of foreign words, and therefore Gibbs could tell, without any help from Covey,

[69

whether these Africans were speaking a native language or one mixed with Spanish. So ended the first day's proceedings.

Next morning, the Court admitted Dr. Gibbs's testimony—"not as corroborative of Covey." Covey, who was addressed by the court and lawyers as "James," gave a brief account of his life, in order to explain how he came to speak Mende. Then Cinque was called and Covey interpreted for him. The clerk read the oath and Covey repeated it to Cinque in Mende. Cinque told his story, from the landing in Havana until the capture of the *Amistad* off Long Island. "He manifested a high degree of sagacity, of keenness and decision," reported the New Haven *Herald*. "The wonderful expression of his countenance, as he gave a negative to the question of Gen. Isham [Lieutenant Gedney's lawyer] whether the brutality to which they were subjected on board the *Amistad* before their rising was not in sport, spoke a language which met an audible response from the entire assemblage."

Dr. Madden's deposition was introduced. In the afternoon the examination of the Africans continued. Cinque and his right-hand man, Grabeau, told once more that the captain had killed one of their number with a knife before being killed himself; that they had been whipped and beaten by captain and sailors, and that the cook had told them that they were to be killed and eaten. "Grabeau showed the position in which they were forced to remain aboard the slaver," reported the *Herald*. It was a half-crouching position that caused great discomfort, but enabled the slave trader to pack more bodies in the available space. "The old maxim that actions speak louder than words is true in more senses than one. When Cinque placed himself in this same position in the morning, his action induced an instantaneous silence and solemnity in the assemblage, which the highest eloquence of language might well covet as its richest reward."

The counsel for Lieutenant Gedney now attempted to call the Marshal, Mr. Norris Wilcox, to testify that Covey had told him that Cinque had admitted to having been a slave trader in Africa. The defense objected, and Judge Judson ruled that Lieutenant Gedney's counsel might ask Covey, on cross-examination, whether "Cinque had said anything like that and whether he, Covey, had told the Marshal so . . . and if he answered in the negative, that the testimony of the Marshal might be introduced to contradict the interpreter only." Covey denied having said—to the Marshal or to anyone else—that Cinque was a slave trader. Apparently, the question was regarded as a critical one by both sides, for a whole day was taken up in discussing it.

The *Herald* objected that "much time was wasted and great confusion produced" because the lawyers used language too difficult for Covey to understand. For example: "James, tell him [Cinque] to detail minutely all the particulars relating to the manner of his captivity." To which the response was, "Sir?"

The Marshal testified that on the day that Covey arrived at the jail, "I told James to ask Cinque how he came to be taken and sold. He did so. Cinque replied, as James interpreted it, that he owed a man two pounds—holding up two fingers—to pay this he sold to him two negroes—one ran away. The man then called for the one pound—he had no other negro, and therefore turned out clothing, as security. The man turned the clothing over to another, who called upon him for payment, but he being unable to pay, the person sold *him*." Cinque was further quoted as saying that aboard the *Amistad* "he had plenty to eat and drink and they took good care of him."

George E. Day, one of the theological students who had been instructing the Africans, was called by the defense. He said he had been in the room at the time and had not heard

[7]

any such history of Cinque as the Marshal was talking of. A Mr. Trumbull, of Stonington, had been present and he had put leading questions, "in order to draw from Cinque such a statement, remarking that he had heard such a story, and had no doubt of the fact." Day said that about three weeks later, "I saw such a statement in the *Daily Herald* and that was the first intimation I had that anything of the kind was said."

At the end of the day, the lawyers representing the owners of the *Amistad* moved that the owners might enter bonds in lieu of their property now held for salvage and that appraisers might be appointed. The court adjourned until nine a.m. Thursday morning.

At the next session Dr. Gibbs was recalled and testified that Cinque had "invariably denied that he had ever dealt in slaves." His testimony was, however, objected to and ruled out by the Court. Dr. Gibbs explained that the reason Cinque had been heard to say "if anyone said he had dealt in slaves he told a lie" was because he himself had said to Cinque, "Suppose one of these Africans should say you stole him."

Marshal Wilcox was recalled and confirmed his previous testimony. Colonel Pendleton, the jailer, testified "much as the Marshal had done. From him it appeared that the interpreter might have been in conversation with Grabeau."

The slave boy, Antonio, was called next. In broken English and through a Spanish interpreter he testified as he had in New London and Hartford. He said the slaves had come aboard the *Amistad* with Ruiz and Montes at about eight p.m. (not, as the opposition counsel pointed out triumphantly, "in the middle of the night"), and that the cook had indeed told them that they would be killed and eaten at the end of the voyage. "Here a great effort was made by the counsel opposed to the Africans to draw out from the witness that the threats of the cook were merely in sport." Antonio went on to say that Cinque had thrown the dead captain's body overboard, first taking his watch; that Ruiz had ordered Antonio to throw ship's biscuit among the Negroes when the mutiny began; that Cinque had threatened to kill Ruiz, Montes, and Antonio, as well as Bar-ma, who had taken their part. He tied Antonio by the neck to the anchor. Bar-ma cut him loose. At Long Island, all went ashore except the sick. Ruiz had carried slaves in the *Amistad* regularly for about two months.

IsHAM: What possible bearing can this have upon the case? We are not here to try the captain of the *Amistad*. He is dead.

THE COURT: If Ruiz was engaged in that business, must he not have known that these slaves were just from Africa?

BALDWIN: We claim that if we show that he was engaged in this illegal business, we make him an accomplice with the persons who imported these slaves from Africa.

On Thursday afternoon District Attorney Holabird presented the papers of the *Amistad,* and depositions from crew members of the *Washington,* describing the capture. The defense then brought forward a Mr. Francis Bacon, of New Haven, who had been on the West African coast in July 1839, and knew the island of Lomboko; in fact, he had been a house guest of Don Pedro Blanco, owner of Lomboko's "slave factory." Bacon said that Lomboko was frequented by Havana traders, and that he had seen American, Russian, Spanish, and Portuguese ships in the river there. The slave trade, he said, was "the universal business of the country, by far the most profitable." Slaves were brought to the coast by other blacks, as no white man would dare go inland. Some black men, educated at Sierra Leone, were big slave traders at Lomboko. At the end of his testimony, Mr. Bacon said that he hoped nothing he had said would prove injurious to Don Pedro Blanco, who had been a charming host. (As a matter of fact, Lomboko had been raided by the British about a month before, all the slaves there liberated, and Don Pedro put out of business. He retired a millionaire.)

On Friday morning Mr. Holabird introduced a statement from the Spanish consul in Boston, which said that the consul knew of no law *in force* in Cuba against the importation of African slaves. One of Gedney's lawyers said that since the Africans had committed a crime in Spanish waters, they must be handed over to Spain for punishment; but that in any event, his client was entitled to salvage rights. Governor Ellsworth, representing Captain Green, said that he would not advocate giving up the Africans, but that in any event *his* client was entitled to salvage rights, because he had performed "more valuable and hazardous service" than the officers of the *Washington*, and therefore his right was "paramount." The counsel for the Havana owners said that since Gedney and Meade were in the service and pay of the United States they should render assistance without compensation; and that as Captain Green had not saved the vessel and cargo but had merely made an attempt to do so, his claim was even less valid.

On Friday afternoon Messrs. Baldwin, Sedgwick, and Staples each spoke, summing up the case for the Africans: Every human being is born free, unless the contrary can be proved; these Africans were born free. They were not subjects of Spain, nor were they subject to Spanish law while on Long Island. In subduing Montes and Ruiz, they had quite properly taken possession of their just rights. If they were not slaves when they set foot on American soil, they could not be pronounced slaves now. They were being held illegally. No foreign government could enter our limits and take a person hence. "The interference of the Spanish minister in this case . . . is an insult to our Government."

ON TRIAL IN NEW HAVEN

At a short session on Saturday, Gedney's lawyer, General Isham, wished to make it clear that his client did not ask for salvage "on human flesh," but only asked a reasonable compensation for preserving the owners' property.

Judge Judson handed down his decision on Monday morning. The courtroom was packed, and, despite the continuing cold, a large overflow crowd stood outside, stamping their feet to keep warm and waiting for those lucky enough to get inside to pass the news out to them.

The Judge divided his decision into seven points:

1. The Court had jurisdiction in the case, since the whole affair had taken place on the high seas.

2. Lieutenant Gedney and his companions were entitled to salvage on the vessel and goods in the amount of one-third of the appraised value. The vessel and goods should be delivered to the Spanish government as soon as this payment had been made.

3. There could be no salvage rights on the Africans, since under the laws of Connecticut slaves had no value and were not salable.

4. Captain Green was not entitled to salvage because he was never aboard the *Amistad*.

5. The slave Antonio, having been born in Cuba, should be restored to his owner, under the terms of the Treaty of 1795.

6. The Africans were neither slaves nor Spanish subjects.

7. "Free by the law of Spain itself," the prisoners were to be "delivered to President Van Buren for transport back to Africa, under the statute of 1818, regarding slaves illegally in the United States in violation of an act of 1808, prohibiting the slave trade."

Judge Judson added solemnly, "Cinque and Grabeau shall not sigh for Africa in vain. Bloody as may be their hands, they shall yet embrace their kindred."

[75

7

MR. ADAMS TAKES THE CASE

Judge Judson's decision that the "Amistads" should be returned to Africa caused astonishment on both sides. The newspapers fulminated or rejoiced. The Africans themselves trooped back to the county jail, grateful not to be hanged but puzzled as to why they were not at once on their way home. The U.S.S. *Grampus* sailed out of New Haven harbor; President Van Buren was reported by those close to him to be "greatly dissatisfied"; and Mr. Holabird, in dismay, immediately appealed the case. The appeal would not come up until April, and meanwhile the tutors from Yale Divinity School were delighted to have more time in which to prepare their charges to carry the Gospel to Africa.

As soon as the trial was over, John Quincy Adams put through a resolution in the House directing that all the official correspondence in the *Amistad* matter—or as much of it as Mr. Forsyth saw fit to allow—should be published as a House Document. The Antislavery Depository printed ten thousand copies, and they were soon sold out. Because of a mistranslation, the document made the Africans' case appear weaker than it actually was: the word *ladinos*—meaning Negroes born in Cuba before 1820—was rendered into English as "sound negroes." Adams demanded and got a Congressional investigation to ascertain how this mistake had occurred. A clerk in the Government Printing Office took the blame for it, and no higher persons appeared to be involved.

Public interest in the case remained high, although the last moments of the New Haven trial were driven off the front pages by the sinking of the steamboat *Lexington* in Long Island Sound—one of the great disasters of our maritime history, and the subject of one of Currier and Ives's most famous lithographs.

In April, just before the case was to come before Judge Thompson in the Circuit Court, John Calhoun proposed two resolutions in the Senate, which were unanimously adopted. They were carefully worded, so as not to offend Northerners —it was an election year—but it was clear what his purpose was:

> 1. Resolved—that a ship or vessel on the high seas, in time of peace, engaged in a lawful voyage, is according to the laws of nations under the exclusive jurisdiction of the state to which her flag belongs, as much so as if constituting a part of its own domain.
> 2. Resolved—that if such ship or vessel should be forced, by stress of weather, or other unavoidable cause into the port, and under the jurisdiction of a friendly power, she and her cargo, and persons on board, with their property, all the rights belonging to their personal relations, as established by the laws of the state to which they belong, would be placed under the protection which the laws of nations extend to the unfortunate under such circumstances.

In the House Mr. Adams tried and failed to put through a resolution declaring that the Africans of the *Amistad* were being detained unlawfully. He was quick to point out that the second Calhoun resolution inadvertently supported the Africans' case, for surely, as citizens of an independent government (Mendeland) they were deserving of the "protection which the laws of nations extend to the unfortunate."

Adams had still not taken an active part in the defense of the Amistads, but his diary and his private correspondence show that it was much in his thoughts. He had let it be known publicly that he thought the prisoners ought to have been released on habeas corpus, and his opinion gave stature and respectability to the whole matter; for even in the eyes of those who did not agree with him Mr. Adams was an august old statesman. Nicholas Trist came to see him in Washington, leaving a mountain of papers supposed to prove that his behavior as American consul in Havana had been irreproachable. Adams kept the papers for a while, but then gave them back, confiding to his diary that he had left them largely unread. He did not join in a demand for a Congressional investigation of Trist—perhaps out of respect for the family of Thomas Jefferson—but he had no use for the man. Nicholas Trist, he said, was guilty of "either the vilest treachery or the most culpable indifference to his duties."

When the appeal came before Judge Thompson, in April 1840, Roger Baldwin argued that it should be dismissed on the grounds that the government had no right or interest in the case. The judge ruled that while the government could not "dictate or direct the Court, . . . the question now has become one between the two Governments (Spain and the United States) and its importance demands the decision of the Supreme Court."

The justices having agreed to hear the case, it was put on the Supreme Court's agenda for the following January. More commodious quarters for the prisoners had at last been found in the village of Westville, just outside New Haven, and there they remained, in good health but wistful spirits, attended daily by their mentors from the Yale Divinity School. The jailer, Colonel Pendleton, had taken the three little girls into his own home. The abolitionists wrote that Pendleton had helped himself to three household slaves, while people of a different turn of mind praised his kindness in caring for the children and expressed anxiety lest they become hopelessly spoiled.

Of the three defense lawyers, Staples had quit the case, and Sedgwick was leaving most of it to Baldwin. The *Amistad* committee was deeply concerned lest Mr. Baldwin be unable, singlehanded, to sway the Supreme Court justices, the majority of whom were Southerners. Tappan and the rest of the committee knew that Mr. Adams did not wish to become identified with abolitionists, yet they were convinced that only he could save the case. Known in the press as "the old man eloquent," he was one of the great orators of the day. Tappan sought and received the support of one of Adams' lifelong friends, Ellis Gray Loring, a Massachusetts lawyer, and in October 1840 Loring brought Tappan to call at the old Adams homestead in Quincy. They asked Adams to take the case.

"I am too old," Adams answered, "too oppressed by my duties in the House of Representatives, too inexperienced after a lapse of thirty years in the forms and technicalities of arguments before the Supreme Court. But I will cheerfully do what I have hitherto offered, that is, to give any assistance with counsel and advice to Mr. Baldwin."

But Tappan and Loring argued that it was a case of life and death for the Africans, and that only Mr. Adams would have the skill to win them life. At last, the old gentleman agreed. "By the blessing of God," he said solemnly, "I will argue the case before the Supreme Court."

That night he wrote in his diary, "I implore the mercy of God so to control my temper, to enlighten my soul, and to give me utterance, that I may prove myself in every respect equal to the task."

On the same day his son, Charles Francis, also an assiduous diarist, wrote, "This will be productive of results unpleasant to myself for it must greatly embarrass the political party with which I have undertaken to act." (He was the Whig nominee for the Massachusetts House of Representatives, his first venture into politics.)

At about the same time the *Amistad* and her cargo were sold in New London. Refurbished and given a new name, the "long, low, black schooner" vanished from history.

In November, when the House reconvened, Mr. Adams set out for Washington and, on his way, stopped at New Haven to see his clients. (He traveled by train from Boston to Springfield; to Hartford by another train; and to New Haven by a third.) Mr. Baldwin took him out to Westville, where he found the prisoners living in a room that measured thirty by twenty feet and was almost completely taken up by two rows of eighteen cots. (Not counting the girls, there were now thirty-six of them.) Mr. Wilcox, the Marshal, was present and told the visitors that his charges were in good health, due to excellent care, but too stupid to learn very much. Mr. Adams thought the clothes and bedding could be improved, but Wilcox replied that they were the best available and that no presents from outside could be accepted. While Wilcox stood by sourly, Mr. Adams shook hands with Cinque and Grabeau, saying "God willing, we will make you free."

Back at New Haven Mr. Baldwin entertained the illustrious visitor at dinner, after which the prominent gentlemen of the city came to pay their respects. One of the most prominent was too old and ill to come, so next day Mr. Adams called on him: he was John Trumbull, the painter. He and Adams had been friends in London in the seventeen-nineties. Adams also called upon the widow of Elbridge Gerry, fifth Vice-President of the United States and a signer of the Declaration of Independence. Mrs. Gerry was the last surviving widow of a signer. Then, after delivering a public lecture, "Society and Civilization," the hardy old man took a boat to New York and thence traveled by several changes of train and ferry to Washington.

"The life I lead is trying to my constitution," Adams wrote in his diary. It would have killed most men of his age. His days began at dawn and often did not end till midnight. When Congress was in session, he was almost invariably the first to arrive in the House and the last to leave. Sustained by a bit of bread from his pocket, he worked until eleven or after, and then walked home along Pennsylvania Avenue to his house on F Street, about a mile away.

He never let a day go by without writing in his diary—rather cautiously, one feels, as if he sensed posterity looking over his shoulder. At the top of each page he put a list of the day's callers; there were never fewer than two or three, often more than a dozen. While he was preparing for the *Amistad* hearing, he kept up his work in the House—his chief duty (as he saw it) being to wage continual war against the Gag Rule. Day after day he introduced antislavery resolutions which he and all the other Congressmen knew would be laid on the table without being read or acted upon. When he was in Quincy, he saw his son and other members of his family regularly; kept up a voluminous correspondence; and found time to read history, poetry, literature, science, and current affairs

[81

—whether in English, French, German, Latin, or Greek. At one time or another he wrote, for his own pleasure, studies on such diverse subjects as "The Characters of Shakespeare" and "The Conquest of Ireland." A contemporary who paid him a visit at his quiet, old-fashioned house in Quincy (there were straw mats on the sitting-room floor, two sperm candles on the mantel; the walls were hung with family portraits and prints depicting American political events) reported that Adams conversed with him for four hours, rambling agreeably from medieval architecture to stained glass to the latest sculpture in Westminster Abbey to Pope's poetry; thence to Sheridan's plays, Burke's essays, and the works of Junius, who, he said, was a bad man but "never equalled as a writer." Mr. Adams (said the visitor) "resembles a substantial wellfed farmer." He had a cosmopolite's appreciation of good food and drink, unexpected in a New Englander of otherwise Puritan austerity. At one after-dinner gathering of old cronies, fourteen different vintages of port and Madeira were introduced, and Mr. Adams correctly identified each one.

In November "Tippecanoe and Tyler too" won the Presidential election. Van Buren's lame-duck government would still be in office, however, when the Supreme Court heard the *Amistad* case; and no good will could be expected from President-elect Harrison, a Southerner and an enemy of both abolitionism and Adams. In an effort to have the case dismissed, Adams called on Henry Gilpin, successor to Attorney General Grundy, who had died, and on Mr. Forsyth; the argument he made for dismissal was that the United States government was not a party to the case and therefore had no right to appeal from Judson's decision. But, as Adams must have expected, both were adamant: the *Amistad* case must be reviewed by the Supreme Court.

In January Adams received a call from a sister-in-law of

Lieutenant Gedney. She told him that Gedney had been ill, and she had therefore come to beg Mr. Adams not to be hard on him. As it turned out, Adams was not particularly hard on Gedney, but this was probably because he regarded the salvage claim as one of the minor aspects of the case. Certainly he did not believe in sparing if sparing was undeserved, and in this principle he began with his country. When, in 1816, Stephen Decatur's famous toast to "our country, right or wrong," was reported in the papers, Adams wrote, "I can never join with my voice in the toast which I see in the papers attributed to one of our gallant naval commanders. I cannot ask of Heaven success, even for my country, in a cause where it should be in the wrong."

Also in January Mr. Adams received two letters, hand-written by two of the Africans, Ka-le and Kin-na.

Dear Friend Mr. Adams [wrote Ka-le]
I want to write a letter to you because you love Mendi people and you talk to the Great Court. We want to tell you one thing. Jose Ruiz say we born in havanna, he tell lie . . . we all born in Mendi—we no understand Spanish language . . . we want you to ask the court what we have done wrong. What for Americans keep us in prison. Some people say Mendi people crazy dolts because we no talk American language. Americans no talk Mendi. American people crazy dolts? They tell bad things about Mendi people and we no understand. . . . Dear friend Mr. Adams you have children and friends you love them you feel very sorry if Mendi people come and take all to Africa. . . ."

Kin-na's letter was along similar lines:

. . . Judge Judson say you be free, but Government say No . . . If man have knife and come to American people and say I kill I eat what America people do? . . . Dear friend

BLACK ODYSSEY

> Mr. Adams we love you very much we ask we beg you to tell court let Mendi people be free. . . .

Of the nine Supreme Court justices, only two were at all likely to feel even a slight emotional bias in the Africans' favor. They were Smith Thompson of New York, who had presided over the Circuit Court at Hartford when the case was first heard, and Joseph Story, of Marblehead and Salem. Both were old men, whose appointments dated from before the Jackson era. Of the others all but one had been appointed during the Jackson administrations. Chief Justice Roger B. Taney, of Maryland (who, eighteen years later, would read the fateful Dred Scott decision), had been Attorney General and Secretary of the Treasury under Jackson. He was a colonizationist, who had emancipated his own slaves and sent them off to Liberia; he was known to believe that as long as large numbers of Negroes remained in the United States slavery must remain as well.

John McLean, of Ohio, had been Postmaster General when Adams was President. Adams considered him "efficient, but treacherous and doubledealing." He opposed both slavery and abolition. Henry Baldwin, of Pennsylvania, was generally regarded as an eccentric and unpredictable; there were even rumors that he was subject to fits of insanity. James Moore Wayne was a Georgia slaveholder; Philip P. Barbour, of Virginia, was a former Congressman and a strong states-rights man. Adams had once called him "a shallow-pated wildcat." John Catron, of Tennessee, had served under Jackson in the War of 1812. He was appointed to the bench by Van Buren. The ninth judge, John McKinley, of Alabama, was absent from the capital and therefore did not sit on the *Amistad* case.

MR. ADAMS TAKES THE CASE

The hearing was scheduled for February 21, but on February 18 Mr. Adams noted in his diary

> a severe visitation of Providence. There was an exhibition at a quarter past eleven, in the front yard of the Capitol, of firing with Colt's repeating firearms—a new-invented instrument of destruction, for discharging 12 times a musket in as many seconds. I rode to the Capitol with Mr. Smith. We had alighted from the carriage from 5 to 10 minutes when the firing commenced. My carriage was then going out of the yard; the horses took fright, the carriage was jammed against a messenger's wagon, overset, the pole and a whiffletree broken, the harness nearly demolished; the coachman, Jeremy Leary and the footman, John Causten, precipitated from the box, and Jerry nearly killed on the spot. He was taken into one of the lower rooms of the Capitol, where, as soon as I heard of the disaster, I found him in excruciating torture.

The coachman died next day. On February 20 Mr. Adams wrote:

> The arrangements had been made for the funeral of my poor, humble but excellent friend, Jeremy Leary, at about three o'clock this afternoon. I walked to the Capitol this morning, with a spirit humbled to the dust, with a heart melted in sorrow, and a mind agitated and confused. . . . I therefore as soon as the court was opened and the case was called, requested as a personal favor of the Court to suspend the proceedings in this case from 2 p.m. today till Monday—to which Chief Justice Taney answered, 'Certainly'.

The hearing began at last on Monday, February 22. In those days the Supreme Court met in a small semicircular

[85

room in the east wing of the Capitol, just under the Senate chamber. High windows let in some light and air, but when the room had its complement of judges, lawyers, and spectators, it was exceedingly stuffy and crowded. John Randolph had once called it "The Cave of Trophonius." Every spectator's seat was taken, and, as had happened in New Haven, there were a number of ladies present.

Attorney General Henry D. Gilpin, a Philadelphia lawyer, opened the case for the government. His chief argument lay in the impropriety of the United States' "going behind" the *Amistad*'s papers to determine whether or not they were valid. This, he contended, was not a function of one government in relation to another, especially a friendly one. He referred to Calhoun's two resolutions in the Senate and reminded the Court that when American coastwise ships, carrying slaves, had been shipwrecked in the British West Indies, the British had always either paid reparations or restored the slaves to their owners. "In what respect were these slaves, if such by the laws of Spain, released from slavery by acts of aggression upon their owners, any more than a slave becomes free in Pennsylvania who forcibly escapes from Virginia?"

The rest of the day, Roger Baldwin outlined the case for the defense, concentrating heavy fire on Gilpin's qualifying phrase—"slaves, *if such by the laws of Spain.* . . ." But even though both Gilpin and Baldwin touched on every point for their respective sides, both Court and spectators were waiting eagerly for next morning and "the old man eloquent."

8

"THIS MOST SINGULAR CASE"

On the morning of February 24, 1841, John Quincy Adams walked from his F Street house to the Capitol and took his place in the crowded Supreme Court chamber. When it was his turn to speak, every eye in the room watched him as he rose slowly, faced the bench, and began, "May it please your Honors. . . ." His voice was thin and almost quavering, but, to quote Emerson,

> the wonders he could achieve with that cracked and disobedient organ showed what power might have belonged to it in early manhood. If "indignation makes verses," as Horace says, it is not less true that a good indignation makes an excellent speech. . . . [He] sat all his life in courts and in chairs of state without overcoming an extreme irritability of face, voice, and bearing; when he spoke, his voice would not serve him; it cracked, it broke, it wheezed, it piped;—little cared he; he knew that it had got to pipe or wheeze, or screech his argument and his indignation. When he sat down, after speaking, he seemed in a sort of fit, and

held on to his chair with both hands; but underneath all this irritability was a puissant will, firm and advancing, and a memory in which lay in order and method like geologic strata every fact of his history, and under the control of his will.

In the opening sentences of his *Amistad* argument he said that he derived consolation from the fact that his clients had already been defended by Mr. Baldwin "in so able and complete a manner as leaves me scarcely anything to say." He then proceeded to deliver a one-hundred-thousand-word address, composed with all the care of a symphony and with a symphony's concern for harmony and recurrent themes.

The first of his themes was that everyone in the courtroom believed in justice, which, he said, may be defined as "the constant and perpetual will to secure to every one *his own* right. . . . Another Department of the Government of the United States has taken . . . the ground of utter injustice, and these individuals for whom I appear stand before this court, awaiting their fate from its decision, under the array of the whole Executive power of this nation against them, in addition to that of a foreign nation." Quoting Henry VIII, "Press not a falling man too far," Adams none the less proceeded to castigate the outgoing administration's handling of the case. "The Executive," he said, "in all their proceedings, instead of justice . . . substituted sympathy with the white and antipathy to the black."

He then dealt with Calhoun's two resolutions, pointing out that under the wording of the second Gedney had no right on board the *Amistad* and the Africans were "entitled to all the kindness and good offices due from a humane and Christian nation to the unfortunate . . . Lieutenant Gedney, without any charge or authority from his government, without warrant of law, by force of fire-arms, seizes and disarms them . . .

drives them on board the vessel, seizes the vessel, and transfers it against the will of its possessors to another State. . . . I am not arraigning Lieutenant Gedney, but I ask this Court in the name of Justice to settle it in their minds, by what law it was done and how far the principle it embraces is to be carried. . . ."

In Mr. Adams' opinion the Secretary of State's proceedings were "*all* wrongful from the beginning. . . . In Gulliver's novels he [Gulliver] is represented as travelling among a nation of beings, who were very rational in many things, although they were not exactly human, and they had a very cool way of using language in reference to deeds that are not laudable. When they wished to characterize a declaration as absolutely contrary to truth they said that man had 'said the thing that is not.' It is not possible for me to express the truth respecting this averment of the Secretary of State but by declaring that he has 'said the thing that is not.'"

Next, Mr. Adams dwelt at length upon Señor Calderón de la Barca's first letter to Mr. Forsyth, in which he had referred to the *Amistad* as being "laden with sundry merchandise and with fifty-three negro slaves." Mr. Adams begged their Honors to observe the distinction, because it showed "the universal sense of the difference between merchandise and persons."

Adams' second major theme was the presumptuous and offensive attack of the Spanish minister upon our Constitutional liberties, and his ignorance of our Constitutional safeguards. . . . I will not recur to the Declaration of Independence—your Honors have it implanted in your hearts—but one of the grievous charges brought against George III was, that he had made laws for sending men beyond seas for trial. That was one of the most odious of those acts of tyranny which occasioned the American revolution. . . . I submit to your Honors that if the President has the power to do it in the case of the Africans, and send them beyond seas for trial, he could do it by the same authority in the case of American citizens. By a simple order to the marshal of the district he could just as well seize forty citizens of the United States, on the demand of a foreign minister and send them beyond seas for trial before a foreign court.

". . . One moment [the Africans] are viewed as merchandise and the next as persons. . . . First, they are demanded as persons, as the subjects of Spain, to be delivered up as criminals, to be tried for their lives, and liable to be executed on the gibbet. Then they are demanded as chattels, the same as so many bags of coffee, or bales of cotton, belonging to owners, who have a right to be indemnified for any injury to their property." Mr. Forsyth, said Adams, was guilty of saying "the thing that is not" when he wrote that the Spanish minister was demanding the delivery of these people solely as "*property.*"

Getting back to Calderón's letter, Adams continued, "The next argument that follows is so peculiar that I find it difficult to give a distinct idea of its purpose or application." Calderón had suggested that if the mutiny should go unpunished, American citizens living in Cuba and possessing slaves there would be endangered by further attempted revolts. "I believe, may it please the Court, that this is not a good argument before this court, to determine questions of law and justice by the consideration that there are American citizens who own plantations in the island of Cuba, which they cultivate by the labor of slaves. They own their plantations and slaves there, subject to the laws of Spain, which laws declare the African slave trade to be felony. . . . What would become of the liberties of this nation if our courts [were] to pass sentence between parties, upon considerations of the effect it may have upon the interest of American citizens, scattered as they may be in all parts of the world? . . . It was no proper argument. . . . It was calculated to excite and influence the Secretary of State, not only by the effect to be produced in the island of Cuba, but perhaps also by a regard to certain interests nearer home. But was that *justice?* Was that a ground on which courts of justice will decide cases? I trust not."

Mr. Adams next employed the orator's device of *not* talking about something, thereby calling greater attention to it: "There are a few portions of this letter which I had rather your Honors would read when you are together in consultation than to read them myself in this place. I will not trust myself to comment upon them as they deserve. I trust that your Honors, in the pursuit of *justice,* will read them, as the document will be in your hands and you will see why I abstain from doing it." He was referring to Calderón's threat of ill-feeling on the part of Cubans and Puerto Ricans toward the United States, and to his indirect attack on the British Antislavery Commission and the agents of American abolitionists.

So much for the Spanish minister's letter of September 6. And how should the Secretary of State have answered it? He should have informed Señor Calderón at once that what he suggested was "utterly inadmissible." He should have said that "the United States could not deliver the ship to the owner and there was no duty resting on the United States to dispose of the vessel in any such manner"; that the salvage claim must be decided by the courts; and that Calderón's demand that the President act independently of the courts "was not only inadmissible but offensive. . . .

"The Secretary ought to have done this at once, without waiting to consult the President, who was then absent from the city. The claim that the Negroes should be delivered was equally inadmissible with the rest; the President has no power to arrest either citizens or foreigners. But even that power is almost insignificant compared with that of sending men beyond seas to deliver them up to a foreign government. The Secretary should have called upon the Spanish minister to name an instance where such a demand had been made by any government of another government that was independent. He should have told him, that such a demand was treating the President of the United States not as the head of a nation, but as a constable, a catchpole—a character that it is not possible to express in gentlemanly language. . . .

"The Secretary should also have set the Spanish minister right with regard to the authorities before whom the question was pending. He should have told him that they were not the authorities of the state of Connecticut, but of the United States, the courts of the Union in the state of Connecticut. . . . It was a real misapprehension, which has continued through the whole proceeding to the present time, and it ought to have been corrected at first. And what is still more remarkable, the same mistake of calling it the court of Connecticut was made by Mr. Forsyth himself long after."

But, instead, the Secretary had written a short note saying that he had sent the letter to the President and would be in touch later. And Forsyth never had set Calderón or Argaiz right about their misapprehensions and "insolent demands."

"He has degraded the country in the face of the whole civilized world," Mr. Adams said, his voice rising, "not only by allowing these demands to remain unanswered, but by proceeding, I am obliged to say . . . as if the Executive were earnestly desirous of complying with every one of the demands. Why does the Spanish minister persist in such inadmissible pretensions? It is because . . . he was not told instantly without the delay of an hour, that this Government could never admit such claims, and would be offended if they were repeated, or any portion of them. Yet . . . for eighteen months . . . an American Secretary of State evades answering any of them—evades it to such an extent that the Spanish minister reproaches him for not meeting his arguments."

Forsyth had asked Calderón to forward any documents, other than the *Amistad*'s papers, that might support the Spanish case. He had written, "I have the honor to request, by the direction of the President, that you will communicate them to me with as little delay as possible." Said Mr. Adams, " 'That you will communicate them to *me*.' What had he to do with the evidence? . . . it was no part of the business of the American Secretary of State to look after the evidence . . . if he had requested the minister to communicate the evidence to the Court, it might not have been exactly improper, but only officious. . . . Your Honors will judge whether this letter is or is not evidence of a determination then existing on the part of the Executive to decide this case independently of the judiciary, and *ex parte*."

The next Spanish letter came from the Caballero de Argaiz, who, on October 3, 1839, asked that the *Amistad* and her cargo be delivered speedily to the Spanish consul in Boston. He referred to "the Court of New London." Forsyth did not correct him. Later, when Argaiz protested the arrest of Ruiz and Montes, Forsyth wrote that the Executive could not interfere in the courts of New York, "the constitution and laws having secured the judicial power against all interference on the part of the Executive authority, the President."

Said Adams, "That is very correct. There is a perfect answer, worthy of an American statesman. But is that all? No." Forsyth had gone on to say that he had asked the District Attorney of New York to see what could be done to get the two Spaniards released. "What is all this?" exclaimed Adams. "May it please your Honors, I will not here enter into an inquiry of the effect of this interference of the Executive of the United States with the Courts of a State. . . . I really do not know, my imagination cannot present to me the compass of its effects on the rights of the people of the United States." Mr. Forsyth "had suffered both Mr. Calderón and his successor to remain under the impression that if their demands were not complied with, for the kidnapping of these people by the Executive, it was not for the want of a will to do it."

Señor Argaiz had found the District Attorney of New York affable and courteous but unable to free Ruiz (Montes had already jumped his bail). In his next letter Argaiz complimented Mr. Forsyth, calling him "enlightened and discriminating," but, "at the risk of being importunate," presented further arguments as to why the Executive ought to interfere with the courts. "It is allowed by the whole world that petitions or accusations of slaves against their masters cannot be admitted in a court," said he. He added that the American courts could have no jurisdiction on matters governed by the Treaty of 1795, and that if the United States Government did not keep the terms of that document, "there can be no treaty binding on the other party." The Executive, declared Señor Argaiz impatiently, ought to have decided the matter *gubernativamente*.

"And here is a word," said Mr. Adams, "used several times in this correspondence, that no American translator has been able to translate into our language. It means, by the simple will or absolute fiat of the Executive, as in the case of the *lettre de cachet*—or a warrant for the BASTILLE—that is what the Spaniard means by *gubernativamente,* when he asks the Executive of the United States, by his own fiat, to seize these MEN, wrest them from the power and protection of courts, and send them beyond seas!"

Argaiz had written, "The public vengeance has not been

satisfied" and "be it recollected that the legation of Spain does not demand the delivery of slaves but of assassins." Adams pounced on this last sentence as a contradiction of the libel filed at Hartford by District Attorney Holabird at the instructions of Mr. Forsyth, which had specifically called the Africans *slaves* and *property*. It gave him the springboard for a deft argument: "In all countries where men are held as slaves, when they are charged with the commission of crimes, the right of their owners to their persons is, and must necessarily be, suspended; and when they are convicted of capital crimes, the right of the owner is extinguished. Through the whole correspondence between the Spanish Ministers and our Department of State, concerning the surrender of these most unfortunate persons, this broad distinction appears to have been entirely and astonishingly overlooked. . . . Mr. Calderón demands that the President should keep these persons all—all adult males and children of both sexes included—in close custody and convey them to Cuba to be tried for their lives. Is it not palpable that if this demand had been complied with, they could not have been restored to their pretended owners, Ruiz and Montes, as merchandise of what nature soever? With what face, then, could the 9th article of the treaty with Spain be alleged to support a demand for the safekeeping and delivery of the captives, not as slaves, but as assassins—not as merchandise, but as men—as infant females, with flesh and blood and nerves and sinews, to be tortured, and with lives to be forfeited and consumed by fire, to appease the public vengeance of the lawless slave-traders in Cuba?"

Holabird, in his libel, had asked that "the vessel, cargo and blacks . . . should be so disposed of as to enable the United States to comply with their treaty stipulations," and had stated that this demand was made at the instance of the

Spanish minister. But (said Mr. Adams) the treaty stipulations concerned the return of property to owners; and, therefore, the court could not have restored "the negroes, as property, to their owners but by denying and defying the real demand of the Spanish minister, that they should be sent to Cuba as criminals." And if the Supreme Court should now reverse the decision of the lower courts that the prisoners should be delivered to the President to be sent home to Africa, what was the alternative?

> Not, surely, that they should be delivered up to their pretended owners, for against that the Spanish minister solemnly protests! . . . He demands of the Executive Administration (will the Court please to consider what the purport of this demand is?)—that the President of the United States should issue a proclamation that no tribunal of the United States has the right to institute proceedings against the *subjects of Spain* for crimes committed on board a Spanish vessel, and in the waters of the Spanish territory.

At the time that the Spanish minister was making these demands, the Africans were in custody, charged with piracy and murder. They were also being claimed as property. A treaty had been invoked "to sustain the claim that they were merchandise rescued out of the hands of pirates or robbers (that is to say, out of the hands of *itself*) and should be restored *entire*" to their alleged owners. Clearly, said Mr. Adams, the Ninth Article of the Treaty of 1795 could not refer to human beings, since it spoke of merchandise that must be restored entire: "A stipulation to restore human beings *entire* might suit two nations of cannibals." Furthermore, how could the Africans be, simultaneously, "merchandise rescued out of the hands of pirates and robbers and the pirates or robbers out of whose hands the merchandise was rescued?"

"The old man eloquent" now reached one of the most eloquent parts of his address: "The demand of the Spanish minister, Calderón, was that the President of the United States should first turn man-robber; *rescue* from the custody of the Court, to which they had been committed, these forty-odd Africans . . . next turn jailer, and keep them in his close custody, to prevent their *evasion;* and lastly, turn catchpole and convey them to the Havana, to appease the public vengeance of the African slave-traders of the barracoons.

"Is it possible to speak of this demand in language of decency and moderation? Is there a law of Habeas Corpus in the land? Has the expunging process of black lines passed upon these two Declarations of Independence in their gilded frames?" [These hung on the walls of the room.] "Has the fourth of July, '76, become a day of ignominy and reproach? . . . And is it for this Court to sanction such monstrous usurpation and Executive tyranny as this at the demand of a Spanish minister? And can you hear, with judicial calmness and composure, this demand of despotism, countenanced and supported by all the Executive authorities of the United States, though not yet *daring* to carry it into execution?"

A few weeks before the Supreme Court hearing, the British minister, Mr. Fox, had written to Mr. Forsyth, pointing out that England had paid Spain a large sum of money on condition that she would outlaw the slave trade, and that his country "is moved to take a special and peculiar interest in the fate of these unfortunate Africans." He also called attention to Article 10 of the Treaty of Ghent, under which the United States and England agreed to cooperate to end the slave trade. Mr. Forsyth had sent a much more brusque reply to this letter than he had ever given to any appeal from the Spanish minister. "You must be aware, sir," he had written, "that the Executive has neither the power nor the disposition to control the proceedings of the legal tribunals when acting within their own appropriate jurisdictions."

"How quick to perceive an impropriety!" exclaimed Mr. Adams. "How alive to the honor of the country—much more so, indeed, than the case required. How different his course from that pursued toward the Spanish minister, who had been from the beginning to the end pressing upon our government demands the most inadmissible, the most unexampled, the most offensive, and yet received from the Secretary no answer, but either a prompt compliance with his requirement, or a plain demonstration of regret that compliance was impracticable."

In one of his letters to Argaiz, Forsyth had said, "It is not apprehended that the delay will affect the course which the Government of the United States may think it fit ultimately to adopt." Said Adams, "The Spanish minister is here given to understand, in his ear, that care had been taken to prevent the Africans from being placed beyond the control of the Executive." It was clear, he added, that many things must have been discussed between Forsyth and Argaiz that were not made public. For example, in a letter written on December 25, 1839, in anything but a Christmas spirit, Argaiz had reminded Forsyth of a private conversation in which Forsyth had sympathized with him over the arrest of Montes and Ruiz and had said that the two Spaniards were "victims of an intrigue."

"What the Secretary means by 'victims of an intrigue' is not for me to say," said Adams. "These Spaniards had been sued in the courts of the state of New York by some of my clients, for alleged wrongs done to them on the high seas—for cruelty, in fact, so dreadful, that many of their number had actually perished under the treatment. These suits were commenced by lawyers of New York—men of character in their profession. Possibly they advised with a few other individuals —fanatics, perhaps, I must call them, according to the general application of language, but if I were to speak my own language in my own estimate of their character, so far as concerns this case, and confining my remarks exclusively to this present case, I should pronounce them the FRIENDS OF HUMAN NATURE—men who were unable to see these, their fellow men, in the condition of these unfortunate Africans, seized, imprisoned, helpless, friendless, without language to complain, without knowledge to understand their situation or the means of deliverance. . . . These are the men, whom the American Secretary of State arraigns in a confidential conversation with the minister of Spain, as the instigators of 'an intrigue' of which he holds these disappointed slave-holders to be the unfortunate victims."

It was now half-past three in the afternoon, and the Chief Justice adjourned the court until the following morning. That night Mr. Adams noted in his diary, "I spoke four hours and a half, with sufficient method and order to witness little flagging of attention by the Judges or the auditory."

9

VERDICT

But when the next morning's session came, Chief Justice Taney rose to announce, in a shaken voice, that Justice Barbour, of Virginia, had died during the night. A slave, going to awaken him as usual, had found him dead, apparently of a stroke. The court was therefore adjourned for a week. Justice Barbour's funeral was held in the Supreme Court chamber.

When the hearing was resumed on March 1, Mr. Adams again took the floor, and after appropriate remarks about the sad event in their midst and a short review of his chief arguments of the week before, he plunged again into his oration, touching first on Dr. Madden's testimony. "He [Dr. Madden] certainly does not charge the Captain General with bribery, although he says that both he and the other authorities of Cuba are in the habit of winking or conniving at the slave trade. That this is the actual state of affairs, I submit to the Court as a matter of history. And I call the attention of the Court to this fact, as one of the most important points of this case."

VERDICT

With obvious glee Mr. Adams pounced on Argaiz's idea that Ruiz should have been released by the New York court because he had been named in the arrest order as "Pipi" instead of "Pepe." "The argument is certainly ingenious and if it is sound at all, it is worth more in favor of the Africans than of the Spaniards" (a reference to the Africans' fictitious Spanish names as set forth in the *Amistad's* papers). And he waxed very sarcastic about Forsyth's concern that the poor wretches, the Africans, ought to have the opportunity to prove in a Spanish court that they are free by the laws of Spain. ". . . how could that be credited . . . when it is apparent that, by sending them back in the capacity of slaves, they would be deprived of all power to give evidence at all in regard to their freedom!"

A large part of his remarks were directed against Attorney General Grundy's opinion of the case. Grundy, Adams pointed out, had assumed throughout his opinion that the Negroes were slaves and had cited Wheaton's *Elements of International Law* to support his theory that the ship's papers were to be taken at face value and should not be questioned by other nations. But, said Adams, "the voyage of the *Amistad*, for which these papers were given, was but the continuation of the voyage of the slave trader. . . . The Executive may send the men to Cuba, to be sold as slaves, to be put to death, to be burnt at the stake, but they must not go behind this document, to inquire into any facts of the case." Adams said that one of the papers in question appeared to be a passport, with the name of the Captain General of Cuba not even signed, but printed. No physical characteristics had been filled in; it was evidently a form intended for one person, not forty-nine; and it could hardly have been considered valid anywhere in the world. Furthermore, a passport was not evidence of property. "All the decisions of this Court agree that foreign

[101

papers are good only for that which they propose and purport, but not as evidence of property. And yet the opinion of the late Attorney General rests on that ground." Grundy had cited the case of the *Antelope* as precedent, and Adams now promised to examine that case "to the bottom" and show that it was not a precedent; for one thing, in that case the lower courts had stated that if the slave trade had at that time been abolished by Spain, their decision would have been different. That trade had now been abolished by Spain.

"The late Attorney General," continued Adams, "says 'the courts of no country execute the penal laws of another.' I may ask, does any nation execute the *slave* laws of another country? Is not the slave system, the *Code Noir*, as peculiar as the revenue system or the criminal code? These men were found free, and they cannot now be decreed to be slaves, but by making them slaves. By what authority will this court undertake to do this? What right has Ruiz to claim these men as his property, when they were free, and so far from being in his possession when taken, he was in theirs. If there is no right of visitation and search by the cruisers of one nation over those of another, by what right has this ship been taken from the men who had it in their possession? The captors in this case are Gedney and Meade, the owners are the Africans."

Grundy had said the vessel was not engaged in the slave trade; Adams begged to contradict him. Grundy also cited Article 9 of the 1795 Treaty; Adams had already disposed of this one. Grundy, Adams continued, "now came to a conclusion . . . which it is not in my power to read to the Court without astonishment. . . . Grundy says his opinion is that the vessel and cargo should be delivered by the President to 'such persons as may be designated by the Spanish minister to receive them!'

"I am ashamed!" exclaimed Adams. "I am ashamed that such an opinion should ever have been delivered by any public officer of this country, executive or judicial. I am ashamed to stand up before the nations of the earth, with such an opinion recorded as official and, what is worse, as having been adopted by the government; an opinion sanctioning a particular course of proceeding, unprecedented among civilized countries."

He next turned his attention to the clandestine way in which the President had ordered the naval schooner *Grampus* to be ready to hurry the Africans away to Cuba if they lost their case in New Haven. "The Attorney was directed not to allow them a moment of time to enter an appeal. They were to be put on board of the *Grampus* instantly, and deprived, if possible, of the privilege of appealing to the higher Courts. Was this *justice?* Will this Court inquire what, if that [order] had been carried into execution, would have been the tenure by which *every* human being in this Union, man, woman, or child, would have held the blessing of personal freedom? Would it not have been by the tenure of Executive discretion, caprice, or tyranny? Had the principle once been set and submitted to, of a nameless mass of judicial prisoners and witnesses, snatched by Executive grasp from the protective guardianship of the Supreme Judges of the land (*gubernativamente*) at the dictate of a foreign minister, would it not have disabled forever the effective power of the Habeas Corpus?" This was Adams at his most eloquent. The courtroom sat in awed stillness.

The appearance of the *Grampus* in Long Island Sound waters in January excited "surprise, curiosity, suspicion." Her commander, Lieutenant Paine, was forbidden to reveal his orders, but he had pointed out to his superiors that the ship was far too small to be loaded with passengers for a winter voyage. "He remonstrated in vain! He was answered only by the mockery of an instruction, to treat his prisoners with all possible tenderness and attention. If the whirlwind had swept them all into the ocean he at least would have been guiltless of their fate."

Mr. Adams then went on to discuss an article recently published in the *Official Journal of the Executive Administration*. According to that journal's editors, it had come from the pen of "one of the brightest intellects of the south," and contained a discussion of slavery in the light of the *Amistad* case, which the writer said he regarded as "of the deepest importance to the southern states." Adams believed it had been written for no other reason than in the hope of influencing the Supreme Court's decision. "What have the southern states to do with the case?" he asked irascibly, "or what has the case to do with the southern states?" Picking up the offending journal as if it were dirt, he proceeded to read their Honors "the bright southern intellect's" apologia for slavery:

Property in man has existed in all ages of the world, and results from the *natural* state of man, which is war. When God created the first family and gave them the fields of the earth as an inheritance, one of the number in obedience to the impulses and passions that had been implanted in the human heart, rose and slew his brother. This universal nature of man is alone modified by civilization and law. War, conquest, and force have produced slavery, and it is state necessity and the internal law of self preservation that will ever perpetuate and defend it.

"Is that a principle recognized by this Court?" inquired Mr. Adams, and he once more pointed to a framed copy of the Declaration of Independence on the wall of the chamber. "Is it the principle of that *declaration?* . . . If this principle is sound, it reduces to brute force all the rights of man. . . . No man has a right to life or liberty, if he has an enemy able to take them from him. . . . Now I do not deny that the only principle upon which a color of *right* can be attributed to the condition of slavery is by assuming that the natural state of man is War. The bright intellect of the south clearly saw, that without this principle for a corner-stone, he had no foundation for his argument. . . . The moment you come to the Declaration of Independence, that every man has a right to life and liberty, an inalienable right, this case is decided. I ask nothing more in behalf of these unfortunate men than this Declaration."

After a recess for lunch, Mr. Adams devoted more than an hour to a very minute examination of the *Antelope* case, with the conclusion that it offered no precedent for the matter before the Court. Before resting the case, he said a few personal words that touched all who heard them, regardless of how they felt about the *Amistad:*

"May it please your Honors: On the 7th of February, 1804, now more than thirty-seven years past, my name was entered, and yet stands recorded, on both the rolls, as one of the Attorneys and Counsellors of this Court. Five years later, in February and March, 1809, I appeared for the last time before this Court, in defence of the cause of justice, and of important rights, in which many of my fellow-citizens had property to a large amount at stake. Very shortly afterwards, I was called to the discharge of other duties—first in distant lands, and in later years, within our own country, but in different departments of her Government. Little did I imagine that I should ever again be required to claim the right of appearing in the capacity of an officer of this Court; yet such has been the dictate of my destiny—and I appear again to plead the cause of justice, and now of liberty and life, in behalf of many of my fellow men, before that same Court, which in a former age, I had addressed in support of rights of property. I stand again, I trust for the last time, before the same Court—*hic caestus, artemque repono.* I stand before the same Court, but not before the same judges—nor aided by the same associates—nor resisted by the same opponents. As I cast my eyes along those seats of honor and of public trust, now occupied by you, they seek in vain for one of those honored and honorable persons whose indulgence listened then to my voice. Marshall—Cushing—Chase—Washington—Johnson—Livingston—Todd— Where are they? . . . Where is the marshal—where are the criers of the Court? Alas! where is one of the very judges of the Court, arbiters of life and death, before whom I commenced this anxious argument, even now prematurely closed? Where are they all? Gone! Gone! All gone!— Gone from the services which, in their day and generation, they faithfully rendered to their country. . . . In taking, then, my final leave of this Bar, and of this Honorable Court, I can only ejaculate a fervent petition to Heaven, that every member of it may go to his final account with as little of earthly frailty to answer for as those illustrious dead, and that you may, every one, after the close of a long and virtuous career in this world, be received at the portals of the next with the approving sentence, 'Well done, good and faithful servant; enter thou into the joy of thy Lord.'"

The lawyer representing the government, Mr. Gilpin, now took the floor with a rebuttal, but his speech was an anticlimax. How could any ordinary man successfully follow the grand old orator? Gilpin took three hours, avoiding any criticism of Mr. Adams' arguments and attacking those of Roger Baldwin instead. When he had finished, the Justices retired and took several days to consider their verdict.

March 9 was the day of decision. Mr. Adams arrived at the Supreme Court chamber early, and waited half an hour alone. Mr. Baldwin had been called back to New Haven. Then their Honors filed in and Mr. Justice Story rose to read the verdict. In the leisurely style of the times, he spent an hour reviewing the facts of the case and then two hours or more in delivering the decisions that had been awaited for a year and a half. In essence, here was the verdict:

Article 9 of the Treaty of 1795 did not apply to the case, for the reason that the Africans were never legally the property of Montes and Ruiz. "There is no pretence to say the Negroes of the *Amistad* are 'pirates' and 'robbers', as they were kidnapped Africans, who by the laws of Spain itself were entitled to their freedom."

The so-called passport, bearing the Spanish names of the Africans, was no evidence of their being slaves or property, because it was clearly fraudulent. "Fraud will vitiate any, even the most solemn, transactions."

Lieutenant Gedney and his officers and crew had performed a useful service, and were entitled to salvage rights. The amount allowed by Judge Judson—one-third of the value of the cargo—"does not seem beyond the exercise of a sound discretion."

When the *Amistad* was boarded by the American Coast Guard officers, she was in the possession of the Africans; clearly, they had not imported themselves into the United States in order to sell themselves as slaves. For this reason, the Supreme Court reversed Judge Judson's decision that they should be returned to Africa in accordance with the antislave-trade law of 1808. Instead, being as entitled to their liberty as any other free-born human beings, they were to be discharged at once. As Adams wrote to Roger Baldwin later that morning, signing himself "in great haste and great joy," the captives were free.

10

LIGHT FOR THE DARK CONTINENT

Lewis Tappan and Roger Baldwin went to Westville together and brought the glad tidings to the Amistads. The whole company was ecstatic. Mingled with lively expressions of gratitude (Ka-le sat down and wrote a thank you letter to Mr. Adams) were eager inquiries as to how soon they might embark for home. Unfortunately, the very generosity of the Supreme Court had worked against their greatest hope, that of going back to Africa as soon as possible. Had the court ordered them to be deported, the government would have had to provide transportation. But they were free. Therefore, funds would have to be raised for their passage. Furthermore, Lewis Tappan and the many other pious people who formed the *Amistad* committee had no intention of simply turning their charges back into the jungle. These elect blacks were to be God's instruments in bringing light to the dark continent, and they still needed more theological training in order to carry out their missionary role.

All this was not easy to explain to thirty-two men who had been detained in a crowded room for a year and a half and knew that they were legally free. Some of them fleetingly entertained the idea of staying in America for good ("America good country," said Cinque. "We think, then we tell"). But in the end, home seemed best. One of the divinity students who had been teaching them, Amos Townsend, reported, "The delay has thrown a gloom over their minds very difficult to be dissipated." Although a few of them seemed to enjoy scholarly pursuits ("Kin-na is the chief stimulator of the others to study"), and several appeared to have become sincere Christians, most were clearly pining away for the life they were accustomed to.

That such a life would have any attraction for men lucky enough to have seen Connecticut was incomprehensible to Tappan and his evangelical friends. They supposed that they were pouring the elixir of morality, religion, and civilization into empty vessels, but the truth was that the Mende had a religion and a code of living that quite satisfied them. If the prisoners said little about it to their kind instructors, it was because much about it was secret. All boys and men in the tribe belonged to a secret society and the women and girls belonged to another. As with Masons and other secret societies familiar to us, there were various degrees of initiation and one advanced slowly over a lifetime, until only the very old and greatly respected knew the innermost secrets. The Mende of Cinque's day believed in a Supreme Being, creator of all, who punished or rewarded. Thus they had no difficulty in accepting the God offered them in New Haven. The Mende God was a more remote and unapproachable figure than the God of the Christians. However, he could be approached "through channels," as it were: one's immediate ancestors could be asked to convey a petition to a more remote ancestor, who told it to the spirits of the hills and water, who told it to God (Ngewo). Ngewo dwelt in the sky, far away, but the forests and streams were full of spirits who kept an eye on all that was going on. Some of the spirits were of a benign nature, like saints and angels, but most were either unpredictable, like djinn, or evil, like devils. They had to be propitiated with rituals and offerings; for while a man with a clear conscience stood a better chance of staying out of their way, it was clear that calamity could overtake even the best-behaved.

Christian Americans were shocked by belief in magic, witchcraft, and the propitiation of supernatural powers, perhaps forgetting that such things had been everyday facts of life to their own revered colonial grandfathers. As for polygamy, it seemed to show unbridled sensuality. Seeking to learn all they could about life in Africa, the members of the *Amistad* committee came upon a book written in 1837 by a Frenchman, J. H. Guenebault, which confirmed their worst suspicions. "Negroes and Negresses both exhibit great lasciviousness," said Guenebault, "though the latter carry it to an extent unknown in our climates. . . . Almost all travellers in Africa maintain . . . that Negroes are more captivated by white women than by Negresses; which seems to be a proof of the superiority of our race." He went on to say that besides having no religion and no morals, the black race possessed no art, no games, no buildings, no music, no political institutions, and only the most primitive language. "Time and space have not been wanting to the African, yet he remains in a stupid and brutish state; whilst the other nations on earth have approached more or less to social perfection."

Other writers argued that the life of a savage in his native land, lying under a tree and eating coconuts as they dropped, was idyllic, and that it was not only impossible but undesirable to civilize him. Cinque and his friends could have told them that staying alive in the West African hinterland required hard work and ingenuity. A Mende community, which consisted of compounds of extended families, faced the problems of poor soil, encroaching jungle growth, marauding animals, disease, and slave hunters. At the time of the *Amistad* Africans, the last were the greatest hazard of all. Towns that had once been well organized and prosperous had been demoralized by years of unpredictable attack. German villages during the Thirty Years' War present a parallel; but the international slave trade had been going on not for thirty years but for nearly three hundred. Before it was over, it took some ten million souls from their homeland.

But in spite of constant disruption—and to contradict the Frenchman Guenebault—life in Mendeland had political organization. The headman of each town was the oldest member of the leading family and was responsible to the Mende chief, who ruled over the whole tribe, spread out over thousands of square miles. He (or sometimes she) had absolute power, but was subject to a code of behavior and held to it by a tribal authority that consisted of the headmen, a subchief, and various other officers. If he overstepped his bounds, he was deposed. Tribute was due the chief in goods and labor; all the land belonged to him, but all the people were entitled to use it for hunting, fishing, and farming.

Among the Mende, as among many other African tribes, there was an intricate system of law; but it differed so much in concept from that of the European that it seemed to the casual white observer to be no system at all. The European believed in written law and in judgment according to precedent. In Africa each case was seen as unique, and it was the object of the court to settle the case to the satisfaction of both sides, with the wronged party entitled not to vengeance but to compensation. Settlement was by agreement, not by decision. Witnesses acted also as jury—a method used among the Anglo-Saxons long ago, the theory being that the witnesses were so intimately acquainted with the litigants and with the circumstances of the case that they were therefore in the best possible position to bring about a just settlement. Prejudice was supposed to be offset by having an equal number of witnesses for both sides. In Mendeland the principals left the court while the witnesses spoke. If these proved equally divided, the case was dismissed.

A trial by these means took a great deal of time, but Africans *had* time. And this was another point of variance with the European who was always consulting his watches and clocks. As a matter of fact, the white man of 1840 would seem inordinately slow to us. Speeches and sermons commonly went on for from two to six hours. Casual visits lasted all day; mothers-in-law might come to stay for six months or a year. A woman thought nothing of spending seven years making a bedspread. Journeys, letters, cooking, engagements to marry—all these things were long. But if Americans of 1840 had more time than we do, the Africans had even more and made the white man tap his foot and call them lazy and dull-witted.

After the Supreme Court decision Cinque confessed to one of his teachers that the Amistads had had a pact to reveal as little as possible about themselves, for they had not known what these unpredictable white men might approve or disapprove. Certainly they were anxious to please, and said "yes" if they thought a negative answer might be unwelcome. But, in any case, Mr. Tappan and his colleagues would have seen little merit in Mende culture even if it had been explained. For them, heathens were bad and Christians were good, and that was that.

One point that the Africans prudently kept still about was that slavery was inherent in Mendeland. The *Amistad* lawyers at New Haven, arguing so earnestly as to whether or not Cinque had been a slave trader, were trying to make a point where there was none. If Cinque was not himself a slave trader, his friends and relatives surely were; however, there was a considerable difference between African slavery and the American kind. Among West African tribes, slaves lived with their masters' families, might marry into them, might be set free, and might even rise to positions of importance. They were not an outcast and debased breed. Their lot might be compared to that of English royalists, sold into bondage by the Cromwellians to labor in the New World plantations; or to that of David Balfour in Stevenson's *Kidnapped*, whose wicked uncle paid to have him sold overseas.

The question of the custody of Mar-gru, Te-me, and Ke-ne, the three little girls of the *Amistad*, brought on further litigation, this time in New Haven county court. The jailer and his wife, Colonel and Mrs. Pendleton, applied for a writ of habeas corpus and so did the *Amistad* committee, in the name of one of the teachers, Amos Townsend. Dark hints of forced labor at the Pendletons' were brought into play. Mr. Townsend won. But when he and a bevy of abolitionist ladies arrived at Westville in a carriage, brandishing their writ of habeas corpus, the little girls clung to the Pendletons and, when torn from them, ran screaming through the snow. Enemies of the abolitionists were quick to note the incident. Said the New Haven *Columbia Register*:

> The gentlemen who have been so active to gain possession of these children and taken them from the friends they love may hereafter with great feeling draw a picture of slavery and its cruelty which takes a child from its mother to be sold to strangers—or of the kidnappers on the shores of Africa, hunting down his prey—and illustrate it by this instance of their own inhumanity . . . the negroes have been quite ruined by their "peculiar" friends and taught to hate work as part of slavery, we shall not be surprised to hear of their becoming perfectly unmanageable.

The abolitionists themselves, somewhat taken aback, said that the children knew no home but the Pendletons' and naturally feared to leave it, cheerless though it had been for them. At any rate Mar-gru, Te-me, and Ke-ne were retrieved from the snow and taken to join the others at Farmington, Connecticut, where a barn had been done over for the men to live in and where missionaries were assembling to work with them. The girls, ensconced in private homes, were promptly renamed Sarah, Maria, and Charlotte.

Antonio, the cabin boy, apparently not as anxious to return to slavery as the Spaniards had claimed, disappeared— "spirited away," the proslavery people said, by Lewis Tappan and his meddling friends. Before he dropped out of sight for good, he was reported seen in northern Vermont and then in Montreal. The Spanish minister, in a rage over the Supreme Court decision, made Antonio the subject of two heated letters to the new Secretary of State, Daniel Webster. Señor Argaiz said that "seduction" had obviously been employed to destroy Antonio's former satisfaction with slavery; and that the United States must deliver him to Havana. He also set forth his government's new demands: indemnification for the loss of the *Amistad* and her cargo, "including negroes," and for losses and injuries suffered by Ruiz and Montes during their "unjust imprisonment." He also wanted assurances that no precedent had been established by the way the *Amistad* case had been handled—or mishandled.

Mr. Webster did not answer until three months later. Then he said that he had consulted President Tyler and that the President felt there was no need for further correspondence on this subject, since decisions of the Supreme Court were irrevocable. "The undersigned," wrote Webster, "hopes that M. d'Argaiz himself will eventually join in approbation of the course adopted." As for Ruiz and Montes, Webster pointed out that the courts were open to them if they wanted to sue for reparation and indemnification. And as to the matter of precedent, he begged to assure Argaiz that the United States would "always endeavor to discharge its obligations with justice and honor." With that he ended the letter, and, he hoped, the case. But Argaiz sent a prompt, long, and very ill-tempered reply. Mr. Forsyth, he said, had assured him that the executive power, not the courts, would make the final decision in this matter. Therefore Mr. Webster should not be surprised at a continuation of the correspondence. The *treaty* obligation should be the supreme law of the land; if not so, then treaties should be made with the judicial power, not with the executive. Señor Argaiz cannot comprehend how Mr. Webster can insist that the United States courts had a right to judge this case, for no nation's courts can have jurisdiction over the affairs of another. Furthermore, in rebuttal to the point that the 1795 treaty does not provide for returning pirates or assassins, he asserts that the writers of the treaty could never have anticipated such a situation as this one, or they would have worded it differently. Señor Argaiz attached to his letter a formal protest from the Spanish government.

But Daniel Webster was quite a different man from the apologetic, eager-to-please Forsyth. He sent no reply at all until nine months later and then only after Argaiz had buttonholed him at a diplomatic gathering and pointedly asked for one. Then he wrote that he had not supposed "a reply was desired, or that any advantage would ensue from further prolonging the discussion." In his opinion the Supreme Court decision had closed the correspondence. He added that Mr. Forsyth never promised that the decision would come from the executive, but from the government—a distinction that Argaiz had still apparently not grasped. The Supreme Court being part of that government, its decision was final in matters within its province. He cites instances when Spanish courts had taken jurisdiction over matters involving foreign nationals and had made their own interpretation of the Treaty of 1795. The United States government had never questioned such decisions, even when it "was inclined to dissent."

"The undersigned," he went on, "will make one more attempt to state the general occurrences of this transaction so plainly that he cannot be misunderstood." And he proceeded, coldly but patiently, to review all the facts of the case. His final word about Ruiz and Montes was that they had "held in unjust and cruel confinement certain negroes who, it appeared on trial, were as free as themselves . . . in the judgment of enlightened men, they will probably be thought to have been very fortunate in escaping severer consequences." Thus Mr. Webster ended, though not forever, the correspondence between the Department of State and the Spanish minister on the subject of the *Amistad*.

To return to the cause of all this diplomatic commotion, the Africans, now generally called either Mendians or Amistads, were installed in their Farmington barn early in April 1841 and bombarded with six hours a day of instruction.

Most of the time, they tried hard to be as patient and obliging as ever. Nevertheless, there were lapses. One of their instructors, a Mr. Booth, wrote Lewis Tappan, "They begin to feel their liberty." Cinque, in particular, was not conducting himself as a future missionary ought. "I met him yesterday running through the streets," Booth wrote, "hand in hand with a wild boy of sixteen, and soon after I saw him in a store with a parcel of dissipated young men." For a shilling he would throw off his coat and turn somersaults or stand on his head. Mr. A. F. Williams, the owner of the barn, also complained about them. "The greatest difficulty we have found with them as yet is they have been accustomed to jump and talk for money. It is getting to be quite an annoyance . . . to have them jumping in the street. . . . Some of the men that decoy them are drinkers."

Even worse, when Cinque, Kin-na, and a few of the rest were taken to sing and read for a group of ladies who were making clothes for them, Cinque absolutely refused "unless he could have three dollars." Mr. Booth finally persuaded him to perform without charge, and the ladies, though somewhat taken aback, went on with their benevolent works, and provided sixty-six shirts, thirty-three bosoms, and sixty-six collars. Thirty-three coats and pants were made by a tailor for $150.

A few weeks later, Williams wrote to Tappan to report evidence of spiritual progress:

> "Mr. Pendleton bad man," says Fu-li. "If he be bad man, when he die where will he go?"
> "Go down, down, Devil," says Cinque.
> "If you be good, when you die where you go?"
> "Up. Up, up to Heaven."
> "I hope Mr. Pendleton be good man by and by," says

Fu-li piously. "I pray for him that he repent and be good."

Some of the others shook their heads. "Mr. Pendleton no good, very bad."

But Fu-li insisted, "I read in the book, if man do me good I love him. If he do me wrong I pray for him."

It was the plan of the *Amistad* committee that American missionaries should accompany the Amistads to Sierra Leone and that they should all settle down together and open the first American mission there, in the heart of Mendeland. There were already American missionaries in other parts of Africa, chiefly in Liberia, but they were all under the auspices of the American Missionary Society, which accepted contributions from slaveholders. The *Amistad* committee was determined to take no such "tainted" money and to proceed entirely on its own. In order to raise funds for the journey and for the proposed mission, it was decided that Cinque and nine companions—those who were the cleverest students, the best singers, or the most assiduous Christians—should go on tour.

The word "show" had, for missionaries, a distasteful connotation, and "lecture" exalted the proceedings overmuch. So the appearances of the Africans, usually in churches, were classified as "meetings." Everywhere they went, they gave the same program. A meeting in Boston was described as follows by Lewis Tappan, writing to the British antislavery leader, Joseph Sturge:

> Three of the best readers were called upon to read a passage in the New Testament. One of the Africans next related in "Merica language" their condition in their own country, their being kidnapped, the sufferings of the middle passage, their stay at Havana, the transactions on board

the *Amistad*, etc. The story was intelligible to the audience, with occasional explanations. They were next requested to sing two or three of their native songs. This performance afforded great delight to the audience. As a pleasing contrast, however, they sang immediately after one of the songs of Zion. This produced a deep impression upon the audience; and while these late pagans were singing, so correctly and impressively, a hymn in a Christian church, many weeping eyes bore testimony that the act and its associations touched a chord that vibrated in many hearts. Cinque was then introduced to the audience, and addressed them in his native tongue. It is impossible to describe the novel and deeply interesting manner in which he acquitted himself. The subject of his speech was similar to that of his countrymen who had addressed the audience in English; but he related more minutely and graphically the occurrences on board the *Amistad*. The easy manner of Cinque, his natural, graceful and energetic action, the rapidity of his utterance, and the remarkable and various expressions of his countenance, excited the admiration and applause of the audience. He was pronounced a powerful natural orator, and one born to sway the minds of his fellow men. . . . Large numbers of the audience advanced and took Cinque and the rest by the hand. . . .

The younger ones have made great progress in study. Most of them have much fondness for arithmetic. They have also cultivated, as a garden, fifteen acres of land, and have raised a large quantity of corn, potatoes, onions, beets, etc., which will be useful to them at sea. In some places we visited, the audience were astonished at the performance of Ka-le, who is only eleven years of age. He could not only spell any word in either of the Gospels, but spell sentences, without any mistake; such sentences as 'Blessed are the meek, for they shall inherit the earth,' naming each letter and syllable, and recapitulating as he went along until he pronounced the whole sentence.

At most meetings, after the speaking and singing were over, the audience was invited to put religious questions to the Africans.

"How do you know you have a soul?" a clergyman asked Kin-na on one occasion.

Kin-na put his hand on the Bible. "This book tells me I have a soul," he said promptly, and added that before he had read the Bible he had been a Sadducee.

"Do American men believe in the Bible?" asked someone in the audience.

"Yes," said Kin-na, "abolitionists."

Kin-na then proceeded to ask the clergyman questions, to the amusement of those present, who seemed to feel that Kin-na's questions were at least as sharp and pertinent as those of the Reverend Doctor.

The touring group was full of spirits, although the routine was exhausting. Like a vaudeville team, they made one-night stands and all-day journeys. In most places they were kindly received. The agents of the Nashua & Andover Railroad let them ride free. The proprietor of Northampton's best hotel entertained them warmly and when they left told them, "There is nothing to pay." Several other hotel- or inn-keepers did the same. At Hartford, when a hotel-keeper refused to put them up, a number of private families took them in without charge. At Springfield they were treated well at the hotel, but insults of a racial nature were shouted at them as they walked through the streets. Kin-na remarked, "We said nothing to them. Why did they treat us so?"

At Lowell they were invited to visit a rug factory, where the workmen collected $58.50 and gave it to the fund. The Africans expressed great interest in the rugs, saying that weaving was a Mende specialty. In aid of their fund, they offered tablecloths and napkins for sale, which they had made by unraveling the edges of squares of linen or cotton and making the ravels into net fringes.

Four hundred dollars was raised in Philadelphia, much of it in small sums contributed by "people of color." Nathaniel Jocelyn had sent his portrait of Cinque to be exhibited at the Artists Fund Society in behalf of the cause, but the hanging committee rejected it, "believing that in the excitement of the times it might prove injurious both to the proprietors and the institution." Farther south than the City of Brotherly Love the Mendians did not venture.

Contributions flooded in by mail. A farmer in Manchester, Vermont, wrote, "Enclosed is three dollars ($3) to help the Mendi people to their home. . . . P.S. I have concluded to make it Five." A lady who signed herself "Widow of an Abolitionist Clergyman" contributed ten dollars, adding, "Should this be acknowledged through the *Emancipator,* please not to designate the State or Town from whence it came." John Jay sent forty dollars collected from "individuals who do not wish their names to be published as the donors." Clearly, the cause was not universally popular, even in the North.

The Amistads who were left behind in Farmington feared that the others had found a way to get home and had deserted them. Morale was low, and even when the travelers returned, the teachers found a regrettable lack of attention to studies and an alarming spirit of insubordination. Someone had given Cinque a coat that did not fit him; he gave it to Bar-ma, bought some cloth, and ordered another coat from a tailor, saying that Mr. Williams would pay for it. On being spoken to severely, Cinque offered to pawn his watch and pay the tailor himself. Still, it was not a pleasant incident. "We have relied on Cinque," wrote Mr. Williams to Mr. Tappan, "to keep the rest in subjection and to enforce our laws and now if we lose him from any means I know not as we shall be able to enforce them. Some six or eight men off today and so did not work or read as we required at regular hours, and so we cut them off from their allowance. They did not like that . . . you know that without order and system our efforts with them will be of little avail. . . . Kin-na has been quite insulting once or twice since his return . . . has become vain, haughty, proud, and self-willed. . . . We now overlook him entirely, seeking aid and council from others so that he may feel that we do not need his services. We think it may humble him."

During the summer, Fon-ne, who was a robust young man and a capable swimmer, drowned in a pond. His companions believed that he had committed suicide. Williams wrote, "I have no doubt that Fon-ne drowned himself. I find that they entertain the belief that they will all die in America; they believe that when they die they will go immediately to Mendi and some of them think the sooner the better." Fon-ne had been visibly depressed for days, and when asked why had replied that he was thinking of his mother. Mr. Booth had made the mistake of reading them a letter from a British missionary, saying that to return the group to Africa would be very difficult and that to set up a mission in Mendeland would be impossible. If the Americans were determined to return them, he wrote, it would be best simply to set them ashore anywhere in West Africa and leave them. From this, the Africans began to lose hope of seeing their native land again.

As the summer wore on, it became apparent that certain citizens of Farmington were less than cordial toward the strangers. On militia drill day Grabeau was pushed into a ditch as he came from buying lamp oil. The oil spilled and covered him from head to toe, to the amusement of his assailants. Cinque then came to Grabeau's assistance and administered a couple of good drubbings. The *Amistad* committee had the rowdies arrested, but the incident disturbed the quiet citizenry and there were those who put the blame on the Africans. By September, even Lewis Tappan was convinced that the group must be sent home before winter. But who was to go with them and to what mysterious shore?

11

MISSIONARIES AND AMISTADS

To find missionaries who were willing to go to West Africa was something like recruiting astronauts today, but more difficult. They had to be not only intelligent, level-headed, resourceful, and courageous to the point of recklessness, but impeccable Christians as well; furthermore, they had to choose between leaving their families for a period of years or taking them along into what it was certainly no exaggeration to term the jaws of death. Lewis Tappan appealed to one after another of the most dedicated and capable clergymen he knew; and one after another they wrote to say that after painful deliberation and earnest prayer they had concluded that their duties lay in their present parishes.

But at last, Tappan's own prayers were answered. He received a letter of application from a man who was not just willing but consumed with passion to go to Africa with the

Amistads. He was a youthful toiler in the Lord's vineyard named William Raymond, and he told Tappan that God had called him in the following manner:

> A year ago last winter as I was laboring in a revival at Woburn, Mass., I had such a view of a world of sinners sinking to hell that for several days I went weeping like a child. When I had been about 3 days in this state I had such a view of the lost world as I never had before. My mind was not directed to any particular part of the world, but to the universal wreck of mind. This view melted my soul in a flood of tears. I cried out, "Lord, what wilt thou have me do, where wilt thou have me go?" No sooner had the words escaped my lips than Western Africa laid as plain before me as though it had not been more than half a mile distant, attended with these words: *"There is your field,"* coming with so much force to my mind as though they had been spoken with a human voice.

As Raymond was unwilling to have anything to do with the Colonization Society ("I considered it antiChristian") or with the American Board of Missions ("with its fellowship with slaveholders"), he formed the plan of going to Africa by himself and settling down in a tribe. "Most of the professed children of God appeared to consider me as visionary," he complained, "and threw all the discouragements they could in the way. I have had it tauntingly said to me as I passed along the street by those in office in the church, 'Well, you haven't gone to Africa yet!'"

Then he heard of Tappan's call for missionaries to accompany the Amistads. In the hope that Tappan would accept him, he went to work in the hay fields and in a wagon shop, trying to earn money to pay his debts, amounting to eighty dollars, so that he could depart with a clear conscience. Besides the debts, there was one more drawback that he felt obliged to mention: his wife was in the family way. "I expect she will be confined in the course of a few weeks. This I know will seem to you an insurmountable obstacle, but be assured the Lord will remove it out of the way or enable me to overcome it."

Anxious to study Raymond's character and qualifications, Tappan hired him, at twenty dollars a month, to teach the Africans at Farmington. Some of the members of the *Amistad* committee, on looking Raymond over, found him wanting in qualities of leadership and advised Tappan to keep the Africans in America until the right missionary should be found. "I don't think Raymond is the man to take *charge*," wrote one. "He is good in his place, but a head man, a sterling man, in every way competent, should be secured to go with them. . . . I think time would give you such a man." But Tappan was now convinced that time had run out and that the blacks must go home as soon as the committee could figure out where home was.

A letter from the Governor of Sierra Leone brought cheer, though with reservations: the party would be cordially received and provided for and efforts would be made to conduct all to Mendeland. The country of the Mende, he said, was about four days' travel from Freetown, but at present was rent by a war between the Mende and a neighboring tribe, the Temne, and was an unsuitable place for white missionaries. He spoke of the destruction of Pedro Blanco's slave factory at Gallinas, but pointed out that the slave trade was far from obliterated.

Mr. Booth went to great pains to prepare a map, taking the outlines of Sierra Leone from a British atlas and filling in the interior from statements made by the Mendians. His task was complicated by the fact that each river had a multiplicity of names—English, Portuguese, and tribal. But even Mr. Raymond might have reconsidered the whole project had he realized the inadequacy of Booth's map.

Soon afterward, Mr. Booth had the temerity to ask for a raise, saying that six hours a day teaching the Africans was very tiring and that he could not continue at twenty dollars a month. The *Amistad* committee thought he was greedy. They much preferred the attitude of Mr. Raymond, who said, "Money is but *trash* unconnected with the glory of God and the salvation of immortal souls." As of October first, Booth was fired and Raymond took his place. The Raymonds now had a newborn baby, and so far it was no obstacle to his work. In fact, the blacks seemed to enjoy the baby. "They take it and hold it, kiss it and sing to it in their native tongue."

By November two more missionaries had stepped forward to join Raymond. One was a former student at Oberlin, James Steele, who came highly recommended by his teachers. "He is a young man of few words but possessing a great deal of energy of character. He is firm almost to stubbornness and yet always appears perfectly willing, nay, desirous, to have his faults pointed out to him." Steele was a widower without children, and he had had experience teaching black people in Ohio. Tappan was delighted to learn that he understood how to run a printing press, for the committee wanted to send one along for printing tracts. These were to be distributed to the heathen as soon as they were able to read. Steele was promptly accepted, and so was a young West Indian "of color," Henry Wilson, along with his wife, Tamar, a former Hartford servant girl whose employer assured the committee that her character was above reproach.

The tours of Cinque and the other star performers brought in nearly twelve hundred dollars; there were more contributions from the general public "for to assist their commity in sending them home [as one man wrote] and in teaching them and their nation the way to Heaven"; and there were also contributions in kind. Besides seventeen baby dresses for the Raymonds, there were plates, glasses, clothing, cornmeal, suspender buttons, scythestones, shovels, pencils, and many other articles useful to New Englanders although not necessarily to West Africans.

President Tyler had ignored all Tappan's entreaties for a ship of the Africa patrol to take the travelers home. In spite of apprehension that the Spanish might waylay an unarmed vessel and seize their prey at last, the committee decided to chance it and, in November, chartered a barque, the *Gentleman*, whose master was familiar with West African waters. The fares for the entire group came to $1840, a sum the committee now had in hand.

James Covey, the erstwhile interpreter, wanted to go along. He had tried to settle down in America, but was not content. He wrote Tappan that he was a "poor boy, no father, no mother, no friend." The ambivalent attitude of many Americans toward Negroes had puzzled and depressed him. One unpleasant incident had occurred in New Haven, when he had been taken to church by some theological students and seated next to white people. Waves of shock had coursed through the city. A letter to the New Haven *Herald* had spoken of "the enormity recently enacted by an African man being seated for two hours in a meeting house right amidst one of the most polished and benevolent societies in the State, to the shocking disturbance of their humble devotions."

Toward the end of the month, a farewell meeting was held in Dr. Noah Porter's church in Farmington. Dr. Porter (a future president of Yale) spoke for more than an hour. Tappan, who had come up from New York, wrote to his English friend Joseph Sturge:

May the Lord preserve them and carry them safely to their native land, to their kindred and home. S-ma, the eldest, has a wife and five children; Cinque has a wife and three children. They all have parents or wives or brothers and sisters. What a meeting it will be with these relations and friends when they are descried on the hills of Mendi! . . . I must not forget to mention that the whole band of these Mendians are teetotallers. At a tavern where we stopped, Ban-na took me aside, and with a sorrowful countenance said, "This bad house—bar house—no good."

The following morning at five, the Africans left Farmington on a chartered packet boat. About a hundred citizens arose before dawn to see them off, "among them some of the first and most delicate ladies in the town." The rowdies who had roughed up Cinque and Grabeau were nowhere in evidence.

The Mendians seized hold of their friends, [wrote an eyewitness] as almost unwilling to leave them, and in return their friends held them fast by the hand; some of the men sobbed aloud. I saw the tears coursing their way down and literally falling at the feet of their friends and in return the young ladies wept, the young men wept, the old ladies wept, and the old men wept, and all wept together and speaking was out of the question. . . . The boat moved off and the interested company lingered—tears continued to fall fast and all was silent. The company tarried yet and as the boat was winding its way and receding from our view among the green hills which surround it, the company moved slowly towards their dwellings to take their morning repast and to bow down around the family altar.

For years afterward, the land around Mr. Williams' barn, where the blacks had lived, was known as Cinque Park. And still to be seen in a corner of the village burying ground is the grave of the drowned Fon-ne.

A final farewell to the American public took place late in November at New York's Broadway Tabernacle. The church was packed, despite an unusually high admission fee of fifty cents. Sarah (the former Mar-gru) read the hundred and thirtieth Psalm. Kin-na spoke in English, Cinque in Mende. There were speeches by Simeon Jocelyn, head of the *Amistad* committee; by Lewis Tappan; and by James Birney, the noted Southern abolitionist, who had freed his own slaves. A Bible was presented by the Africans to John Quincy Adams *in absentia*. The old gentleman was at Quincy, preparing his Supreme Court speech on the *Amistad* case for publication; and, anyway, he had consistently refused to appear with or on behalf of the Africans. He considered that he had done his part; and in consideration of his son's career he wished to avoid as much criticism as his zealous conscience would allow. Thanking the Africans for their gift, Mr. Adams wrote, "It was from this book I learned to espouse your cause when you were in trouble, and to give thanks to God for your deliverance."

The purpose of the final meeting at the Broadway Tabernacle, Mr. Tappan said in his speech, was to show the progress made by the Africans "in civilization and knowledge"; to interest the general public in a mission in Africa; and to raise funds to establish it. There were sixteen Amistads present. One of their teachers called each by his name and he stood up and answered religious questions put by several clergymen. The meeting concluded with rousing missionary hymns—"From Greenland's Icy Mountains," and "Deep in the Desolation of the Race Benighted."

On November 27 the Africa-bound party embarked in the *Gentleman*, and the leading members of the *Amistad* committee gathered in the cabin of the pilot boat for a final farewell. Both Africans and Americans were moved, some to tears, by the occasion. Cinque, in a specially prepared speech in English, promised to keep Brother Raymond and the other missionaries safe from harm.

"Mende people do well," he said. "But not all. Some bad people, same as here."

One of the newspapers commented, "Even those who had often heard him speak before were struck with his pathos, his tenderness, his deep feelings and his powerful eloquence."

Joshua Leavitt recalled the first days in the New Haven jail, when he had brought an old Congo sailor as interpreter—and the deep disappointment they had all felt when the language he spoke turned out to be the wrong one. Leavitt said, "They were then sick, squalid, filthy, uncovered, unwilling to wear the clothes deemed requisite to decency, sad, dark, and despairing." He spoke also of Lewis Tappan's devotion to their cause and of how he had frequently left his business "for many days in succession, at the greatest inconvenience." He concluded by hoping that these Africans would bring to the Mende nation "the blessings of Christianity and civilization." As the steam pilot boat approached the 280-ton *Gentleman* and final leaves were taken, the atmosphere was one of joy and excitement; and there would surely have been toasts drunk if all present had not been such strict teetotalers.

Of the fifty-three Africans who had set foot on American shores in August 1839, thirty-five now looked upon them for the last time. The missionaries and the abolitionists who gathered in the pilot-boat cabin sang about "the pagan in his blindness" and dreamed of a whole continent of black people, each neatly dressed in New England calico and carrying a Bible. If they had known what was to happen instead, their joy might have been mixed with astonishment, and they might have changed their song to "God moves in a mysterious way/ His wonders to perform."

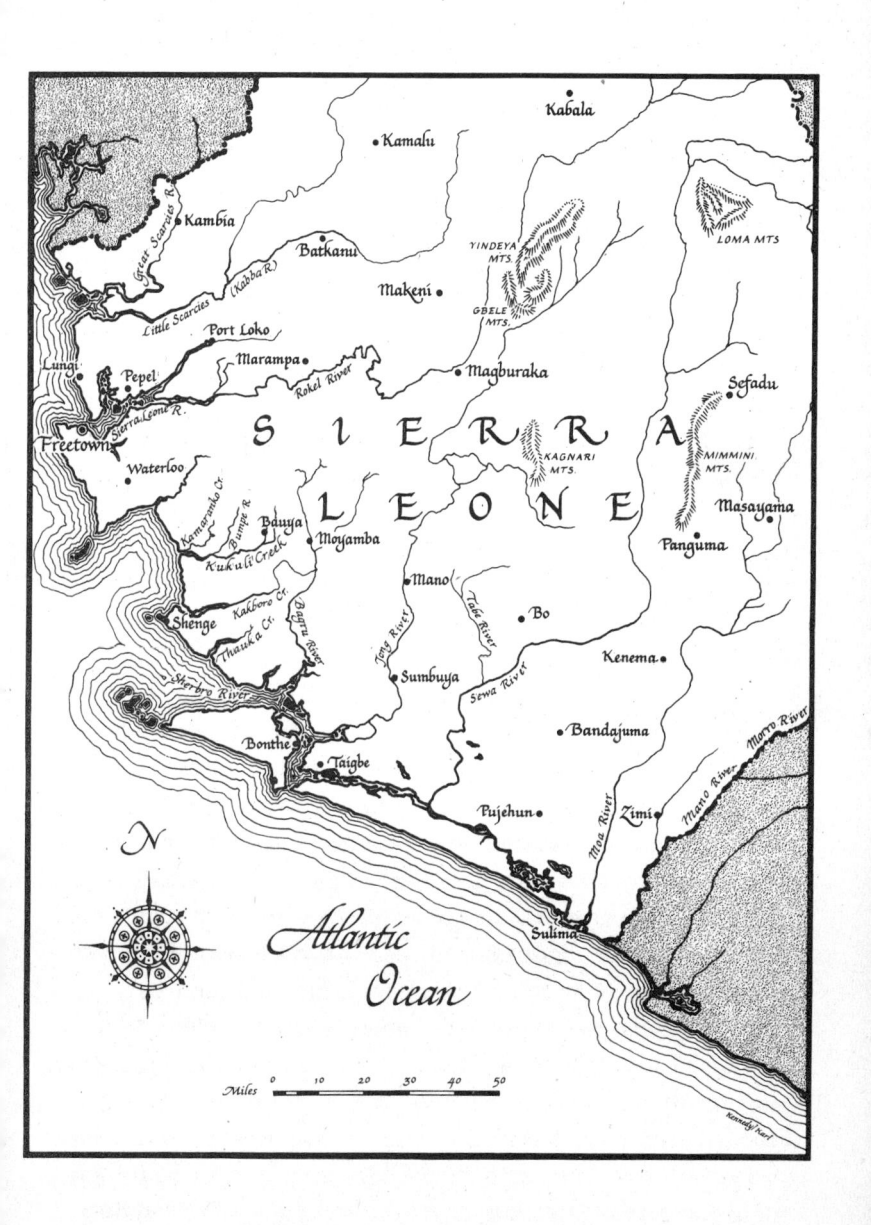

SIERRA LEONE TODAY.

12

THE END OF THE ODYSSEY

After a voyage of seven weeks, the *Gentleman* cast anchor at Freetown one hot and humid day in early January. Sierra Leone has one of the wettest and warmest climates in the world, with, at Freetown, an annual rainfall of 175 inches and a mean temperature of 80. Nineteenth-century New England clothing was incompatible with such weather, and as the travelers approached the shore in a tender they perceived a population going about in the lightest of garments—in some cases "in a state of nature" (to use a favorite euphemism of the day). The homecomers were wearing coats and ties, but when they stepped ashore and found over a hundred Mende waiting to welcome them, it was not long before Cinque and most of his companions began to throw off first one and then another article of clothing. To the missionaries' dismay, they ended by dispensing with their shirts, in order to show their tribal markings. Members of *poro*, the secret Mende society, had certain marks on their backs—the marks of "spirits' teeth." Two or three cicatrices on the cheekbone identified them as Mende.

Some found relatives in the crowd, or heard news of their families. And although they marched ashore in orderly fashion, singing a hymn, they had barely got through the first verse before pandemonium replaced it. There was the wildest excitement and so much joy that Brothers Steele, Raymond, and Wilson decided not to interfere, although this was not the solemn, auspicious beginning to the Christianization and civilization of Africa that they and the *Amistad* committee had planned.

By the end of the day, some of the Amistads had disappeared, and none was in a mood for work. They had been away from their native soil for over two and a half years; they had thanked God daily for their deliverance, had sat through hundreds of long sermons, and sung a thousand hymns. Today they felt themselves entitled to parties and merrymaking after their own fashion. Whether any of them went so far as to enjoy a glass or two of rum is not recorded, but the missionaries were dismayed to observe that Freetown was full of grog shops. (They had also been appalled to discover that the *Gentleman,* despite its passenger list of teetotalers, had been carrying a substantial cargo of rum.) After night fell, the sound of drums issuing from the mud-hut area of the town suggested that heathenish dancing was in progress.

Only now did James Steele, the Raymonds, and the Wilsons realize the immensity of the work of which they were the pioneers. The British missionaries in Freetown received them kindly and acted as their hosts, but gave them no cause for optimism. They believed that the plan of establishing a mission in the Mende country was pure folly. The only possible place for white people in Sierra Leone, they said, was

Freetown, where the adjacent mountain range (named "Sierra Leone" by fifteenth-century Portuguese, either because its outline against the sky suggests the back of a lioness or because the roars of lions could be heard from there) rises to three thousand feet and provides an escape from the hellish climate of the coast.

Except for this mountainous peninsula, which is only twenty-five miles long, the coast of Sierra Leone is low, swampy, and lacking in harbors. The swamps, dense with mangroves, extend inland for up to one hundred miles. In January and February the rains cease, but then a harsh, dry wind called the harmattan blows from the Sahara. It blows for from two days to two weeks at a time, withering trees, splitting doors and shutters, removing veneer from furniture, and shriveling the covers of books. Eyes and throats are dry, the skin peels, and there is an unusual gloom through which the sun, moon, and stars peer forlornly. During the other months, it rains. Violent thunder and wind storms are frequent, the air is always muggy, and mildew runs rampant.

It was true, the British missionaries said, that the inland country of the Mende was somewhat higher and cooler than the coast, rising in places as high as fifteen hundred feet; but there were several excellent reasons for not going there besides the important one that it was in a state of war. First, it was very hard to reach. The mangrove swamps were all but impenetrable; it was necessary to travel by river, braving such deadly hazards as rapids and crocodiles. During January and February all the rivers were too shallow to float even the lightest canoe, and the rest of the year they were wildly turbulent and some became as much as seventy-five feet deep. Another deterrent was that some of the inland tribes were converts to Islam, making the going twice as difficult for

Christian missionaries; for Mohammedanism, with its endorsement of polygamy, its amulets and sacrificial eating ceremonies, was closer to the culture of the people. And then there were the maladies one could contract in the hinterland: yaws, plague, pneumonia, ulcers, rickets, typhus, yellow fever, relapsing fever, meningitis, smallpox, typhoid, worms, pellagra, tuberculosis, leprosy, bilharziasis, and sleeping sickness, to name a few.

Since the founding of Freetown in the seventeen-nineties, the British had attempted ten missions in the hinterland; all but one had failed and that had been abandoned to the French. Perhaps the supreme evangelical effort of the British took place a few years later. It was the Niger Expedition, organized by the Society for the Extinction of the Slave Trade and the Civilization of Africa and prompted by the belief that "nearly the whole of this vast continent, so far as we are acquainted with it, has been from time immemorial immersed in moral darkness, adapted only to exhibit scenes of the deepest human degradation and woe." Four hundred strong and traveling in three iron-clad steamboats, the members of the expedition planned to sail the twenty-five-hundred-mile length of the Niger, dispensing the Gospel as they went—not realizing that only about half the river is navigable and that only in certain months of the year. They did realize that their greatest enemy would be malaria, but the expedition's medical men believed they knew what caused it: "exhalations from the sea water." The deadly element in these "exhalations" they believed to be sulphuretted hydrogen. One of the expedition's doctors wrote, "It is gratifying to know that most likely its influence does not extend to any considerable distance from the sea—and that even there it is not improbable that an efficacious antidote to its destructive effects will be found." Within three months of the Niger Expedition's arrival in Africa, fever had killed twenty per cent of its members and the rest beat a hasty retreat to England.

The American missionaries who accompanied the Amistads also believed in the sulphuretted-hydrogen theory, and sought to combat the deadly fumes by holding handkerchiefs over their noses when on or near sea water. In temperatures that were usually in the nineties by day, they wore flannel shirts to ward off chills. And they slept in stifling rooms rather than breathe any sulphuretted hydrogen at night, when its effects were supposed to be worse. Nevertheless, sooner or later they all became very ill. The treatment consisted of doses of mercury, which caused the patient to develop a wracking fever and salivate profusely. The theory was that two diseases could not exist in a human body simultaneously, and that the death's-door illness brought about by the mercury would drive out the malaria.

While they were in Freetown, however, all except Mrs. Raymond managed to stay fit. On January 27, 1842, James Steele wrote to Lewis Tappan to say that the Lord was looking after them. "Although the men are from different places and even of different tribes, they all propose to settle together. Some of their countrymen who are in this colony propose to accompany them." A few, he was obliged to report, had returned to "former licentious habits." But among the faithful was Kin-na, the best student, who wrote Mr. Tappan as follows:

Dear Sir:
We have reached Sierra Leone and one little while after we go Mendi and we get land very safely. Oh dear friend, pray to God. God will hear your prayer. We will pray for you; and God is very great, very good and kind. We have been on great water. Not any danger fell upon us. Oh, no.

We never forget glorious God for these great blessings. How joyful we shall be. I never forget you. May God be blessed. Our blessed saviour Jesus Christ have done wonderous works. Dear Mr. Tappan, how I feel for these wonderous things. I pray Jesus will hear you; if I never see you in this world, we will meet in heaven.

Your true friend,
Kin-na

Kin-na defected a short time later and joined relatives in the bush. After a few months he was back again with the missionaries. He was to spend the rest of his life trying to combine the best of two very disparate worlds. The better part of his time was devoted to the mission, where because of his intelligence and literacy he was invaluable; but even after he became an ordained minister (as Lewis Johnson) his allegiance to certain aspects of his own culture—polygamy, for instance—caused the missionaries distress.

Steele and Raymond had not intended to tarry in Freetown at all, but to proceed at once, with all their charges, to the country of the Mende. But because of the tribal war, they waited uncertainly for several weeks, and then decided to find a site for the mission somewhere near the mouth of the Boom River, a hundred miles or so south of Freetown. To the missionaries' indignation, Cinque declined to go with them when he heard they were not going to his home. Writing to Tappan, Steele said, "I never talked more severely to a man in my life . . . but I succeeded in accomplishing my object. Cinque . . . said he would go with me wherever I wished to go and wherever I wished to settle he would be content to stop."

While Brother Raymond stayed in Freetown, nursing his wife and trying to keep track of his scattering flock, Brother Steele plunged off across the unknown swamps. He was a brave man. The country into which he ventured was inevitably malarial. Furthermore, the enemies of the Mende, most of whom were Moslem, might capture and take a triple dislike to him, on the grounds that he was white, a friend of the Mende, and a Christian. But if visions of himself in a stewing kettle beset Mr. Steele, he kept them to himself. Holding his handkerchief to his face to ward off the sulphuretted hydrogen, and swathed in flannel, he valiantly struggled across the mangrove wilderness of the island of Sherbro and found a place on the Boom River thirty miles inland and a hundred and twenty miles from Freetown, where a temporary mission could be established until it was possible to move farther inland. When he returned to Freetown, he was suffering from a vicious case of "the intermittents," as the British called malaria. While he lay close to death, cared for by kindly British missionaries, Mr. Raymond and a few faithful Amistads set off with the supplies brought from America to set up the mission. Alas, wrote Steele to Tappan, only a handful of Amistads remained. If only they had not had to stay so long in Freetown, "we should have saved ourselves much perplexity and kept the Mendians from much iniquity." Exactly what that iniquity was Steele did not say—or if he did, Tappan destroyed his letters. Cinque soon relapsed again, for in April Steele writes, "We have freed ourselves from the influence of that villainous Singui who has caused us most of our troubles." Apparently, he preferred a career as trader and businessman to that of missionary. Steele adds that his own health was now so precarious that he had to be carried about in a hammock. "I cannot but wish I had a constitution like my name."

During the spring there was some trouble between the white missionaries and their black colleagues, Mr. and Mrs. Wilson. What caused it has not come down to us, but a letter written to Tappan from his fellow committeeman Simeon Jocelyn, in June 1842, remarks "the case of the Wilsons is indeed afflicting," and they are not mentioned again in letters from Africa.

> I have a painful feeling, [says Jocelyn] in view of the majority of the Mendians now roaming and mingling with the heathen in their sins and degradation after having been so recently instructed in the Gospel. . . . I cannot believe that all these Mendians are to be lost. . . . The righteous are sifted out and who knows but that enough may be sifted out of this little band to produce wonders in the missionary field in Africa. "God moves in a mysterious way," we ought therefore to believe and go forward.

Forward they went, but without James Steele, who decided to go home while he could still walk. He wrote from the ship that took him to England:

> I was sometimes almost ready to wish that I had stayed and seen the end, for if the fever had carried me off, or if I had stayed and died during the rains there would have been abundance of glory in it, and of deep sympathy with me, but as it is having come away and nearly recovered my health I am only barely free from censure. This is not only the award of the public but unreasonable as it seems it is my own feeling.

The mission was now in the hands of William Raymond, who at last had his dream fulfilled of singlehandedly bearing the gospel to the heathen. As he had predicted, his baby had not proved an insurmountable obstacle. It died. Money, however, was an ever-present worry, for neither he nor Steele had been clever about managing the mission's slender financial resources. The printing press they had brought with them was sold for forty-four dollars' profit, but that sum was soon gone, and the day came when Raymond had but six cents left and had to appeal to the British missionaries for help. "O ye Americans," wrote one of them to Tappan, "how can you send forth devoted men and let them starve and die in this treacherous climate?" He added that Raymond ought to have no less than eight hundred a year. Tappan thanked him for his help and advice, but was of the private opinion that the English missionaries lived far too well in their comfortable houses in Freetown. Worse still, according to Raymond, they drank wine—"for weak eyes," one of them told him.

The Raymonds came home in 1843, but only stayed long enough to improve their health and for Brother Raymond to go on a fund-raising lecture tour. He told his audiences that the defection of so many of the Amistads

> was rather an advantage than a disadvantage . . . they have gone through the country as so many living recommendations to me—by their means I am known all along the coast as far into the interior as Cinque has travelled, which is probably 150 or 200 miles. . . . Cinque has settled down in the very town in which we are going to establish our station and it was in consequence of the good account he gave Tucker [a Mende chief] of me that caused him to receive me so cordially and that had he given me a bad name it would have been impossible for me to have got in at all.

This explanation proved generally acceptable. The faithful were generous with money and with such contributions as nails, screws, umbrellas, fishing lines, table cloths, hams, looking glasses, thick boots, and codfish. A Mr. Scovit of Albany sent eight "Colossal Drawings of the Human Stomach," to show "at one glance the legitimate effect of intoxicating drinks upon the delicate organs of the human stomach." A Massachusetts spinster, Miss Ann Harndon, made the supreme gift, herself as missionary. On the voyage back Ray-

THE END OF THE ODYSSEY

mond was faced with a new kind of trial: "The second mate put a very indecent note into Sister Harndon's stateroom window."

A few faithful Amistads had watched over the mission during Raymond's absence. Raymond found everything in good order, but administered a scolding to Ka-le for being too lightly clad and for having sold some shirts that Raymond had given him for his own use. Of the girls, "Margru [Sarah] has done well. I believe her to be a very devoted Christian. Teme and Kene [Maria and Charlotte] have not done well. They give no evidence of being Christians." Raymond now planned an exploring trip to find higher, better ground for a new mission site. Cinque came around to offer to go with him.

> I shall be very glad to have him and all the rest to go with me, [Raymond wrote] but I shall as a matter of course give those who have stayed with me the preference. Of those that are now with me I have more hope of making something than ever I have since we first landed at Sierra Leone. If I can only induce them to marry and settle down by the side of me I think they will be likely to make something. As long as they remain without wives they will be too licentious. Henry Combs, i.e. Lo-ko-ma, is indeed a smart enterprising fellow and I think trustworthy.

Poor Brother Raymond's sanguine outlook did not last long. He could not find the new site he wanted. Sister Harndon took "the intermittents" within a few weeks and died. Raymond's long-suffering wife, Eliza, gave birth to an infant that lived but a few days. After that, she began to suffer from delusions of persecution. She imagined that the Africans were laughing at her and that Sarah wished to make her a slave and turn her out of the house. She also complained of rats in the roof, which was no delusion. Raymond killed a hundred and sixty-four rats in one day, and wrote a plaintive letter to the *Amistad* committee, asking for two dozen rat traps. There was little for Eliza Raymond to do all day but sit in her dank thatched house. In the evening, if it was not raining, she and her husband went for a walk "in our stifling jungle" (as he described it). "The land is mostly covered with small bush so closely woven at the bottom as to be nearly impassable. . . . All of the land in the vicinity of the mission is one vast plain cut up into islands by its many rivers. The country is so level that the tide ebbs and flows up all the rivers many miles into the interior. In the dry season the water of the river at this place is so salt that it cannot be used either for drinking or washing." Sometimes Ka-le (now called George Lewis) and the three girls would paddle the Raymonds along the river in a canoe, singing hymns in time to the paddles. "Sometimes to increase the variety we run a race with some other canoe." After a year and a half, Raymond concluded that Eliza would have to be sent home if she were not to become permanently insane. Sarah, "an active, growing Christian," went with her and spent the next four years at Oberlin College.

Mr. Raymond lasted two more years. During that time, other missionaries came out to assist him, but most promptly died and were buried beside Sister Harndon and the Raymond infants. Raymond suffered from a chronic case of erysipelas but was otherwise in adequate health. He warded off the fever with massive doses of castor oil and lime juice and "was never kept down more than 10 days." He learned a great deal over the years, not the least of which was tolerance. In his first days in Africa, he had banished from the mission any African even suspected of "licentiousness." In the summer of 1844, he had sent away all the remaining Amistads except George Lewis and the girls, "on account of general bad conduct." But they had gradually returned and Raymond became less critical of their shortcomings. In 1846 he was writing Tappan, "Johnson [Kin-na] is still with me and I have told him if he would marry the woman with whom he is now living and by whom he has one child I would build him a house and try to help him. . . . Alexander [Fa-ban-na] has a child by a woman who is a slave." He deplored the cruel ways of the warring tribesmen, but could not but be impressed by the honesty of Chief Tucker, whom he had asked to call his people together to hear a sermon. The chief told him, "I cannot call the people together to hear you talk God-palaver because I am a war man. If I call the people together to hear God-palaver today and tomorrow begin to fight and kill, they will laugh at me." Raymond reported this interchange to Tappan, commenting, "Thus you see this heathen chief could see what seems to be very hard for some Christians to see, and that is that war and Christianity are diametrically opposite one to the other."

Raymond wrote the *Amistad* committee that a missionary must be many things: full of whole-souled pity; a jack of all trades; patient, never arrogant or overbearing toward the natives ("hardly anything will destroy their confidence quicker than this"); kind; sanguine of temperament; and, in short, all things to all men. Despite his Job-like capacity for bearing trouble, Raymond sometimes became discouraged. Once was when his most trusted convert, a man who spent many hours on his knees in prayer and believed he had heard a divine voice saying "love the Lord," tried to seduce Sarah. Another time was when one of the Amistads, Fa, was killed in the burning of a town by enemies of the Mende. Then there was continual trouble with Chief Tucker. To pacify him ("cool his heart," as the local saying went), Raymond so far abandoned his principles as to send him presents of tobacco. Lewis Tappan, at home, was deeply disturbed to hear of mission money being spent for so iniquitous an item.

At last, worn out by his struggles and thoroughly "ripened for heaven," as the missionaries liked to put it, William Raymond died, while on a visit to Freetown, of "the black vomit" (yellow fever). He had outlived or outstayed all the other American missionaries except one, a robust, hell-fire-minded Ohioan named George Thompson, who had arrived a few months before. Another missionary who came with Thompson died eight days after setting foot ashore, but Thompson turned out to be indestructible. He ran the mission for years, outlawing all the little laxities that Raymond had allowed, excommunicating right and left, and cutting off Chief Tucker's presents of tobacco. To Sarah, who was preparing at Oberlin to return as a missionary, he wrote, "I would sooner see a missionary fall dead on the wharf at once than see one walk to this house to set an example of vanity, pride and worldliness. Look to this matter, Sarah. . . . If you have been tempted to get any fine dresses, or bonnets, give them away or throw them away but *do not bring them here.*"

From Oberlin Sarah wrote to one of her former benefactors at Farmington that she was mourning the death of Charlotte, who had died of yellow fever in Freetown two weeks after Mr. Raymond. Thompson had written to tell her of the death, adding bluntly, "Charlotte died without hope." Sarah said that she was hard at work studying algebra, Roman history, and physiology, and added bashfully, "I dare not to tell what [I would like] for fear you will not get it but at any rate I tell what it is. It is accordoum [accordion]. I know you will laugh when I tell what it is. You know that people often says that African people like music." (Despite Thompson's undoubted disapproval, Sarah did get her accordion and brought it back with her to Africa. Several years later she sent it back to be repaired, with the sad notation, "It can't do for our climate here."

Thompson did not get along at all with Kin-na (Lewis Johnson), who had been one of Raymond's mainstays. "He is a very base hypocrite," Thompson wrote the board of the American Missionary Association (which, since 1846, had replaced the *Amistad* committee). "A vile, licentious man, having many wives all about the country. He has tried to do us much harm. Worse than the heathen, he has been excommunicated and is a great trouble to us by his wicked conduct." On the other hand, Alexander Posey (Fa-ban-na) and his wife were church members and "doing well." James Covey, who had been in and out of the mission ever since the return to Africa, came back in 1850, sick and believing himself bewitched. Thompson disabused him of that notion, but had less success in curing his illness. He died and was buried at the new mission, at last established in higher, drier country, according to Brother Raymond's dream. The new mission was named Mo Tappan.

In June 1850 in Freetown, Thompson came upon Tamar Wilson, she who had come to Africa aboard the *Gentleman* with her missionary husband. She was now destitute, diseased, and "knocking about town." Wishing to do her good, and having heard, besides, that she was an excellent seamstress, Thompson took her to Mo Tappan and put her to work teaching sewing, reading, and cooking. A short time later he was writing the American Missionary Association that "she has done but little except lounge on her sofa, and eat—too lazy to try to cure her sores by keeping herself clean. I have found also she is very fond of tobacco and strong drink so I told her I could not have her about the Mission." Neither the cause of Tamar Wilson's downfall nor her subsequent fate are on record. Henry Wilson had long ago returned to America and was reported to be engaged in godly works in New York City.

In due course of time, Sarah finished her studies at Oberlin and returned to the mission, where she spent the rest of her life. Generally speaking, she was a great asset, although Thompson and one or two of his colleagues complained that she was extravagant ("too generous with rice, oil, fish, or whatever she has"), and not a good disciplinarian in the mission school. Once, according to Thompson, she had the temerity to ask for a string of coral beads. Her son by her second marriage was sent to America as a young man in the 1870s. He graduated from Fisk and then went to Yale Divinity School, but died before he could return to Africa.

When Thompson arrived to relieve Raymond, in 1846, he found sixty-eight children studying at the mission; and in spite of wars, misunderstandings, "licentiousness," and the continual need for "cooling the heart" of Chief Tucker, there was never a lack of students. The curriculum included Reading the Scriptures, Writing in Copy-Books, Writing on Slates, Arithmetic, Geography with Maps, Catechism, and Needlework. Thompson was a severe taskmaster—there were even rumors of ear-cropping and flogging under his regime. But still the eager students came.

In one respect, the American mission met with more success than the British ones had ever done. The Americans usually gave a practical demonstration of Christian fellowship, whereas the British missionaries were apt to live apart and aloof from their converts, following what was later to become the British colonial way of life. They directed their attention to the soul almost exclusively. What the convert did in this life, either for a living or for diversion, was not the missionary's business, as long as the convert came to church, wore clothes, and officially renounced polygamy. The fact that the British missionaries were seldom seen performing any manual labor reinforced the African suspicion that labor was an undesirable activity, to be avoided and left to slaves whenever possible. The Americans, on the other hand, often built their own mission buildings and hoed their own gardens. They lived among the people and evinced a desire to help both the converted and the heathen in practical ways unrelated to religion. When, in 1843, the first mission was set up, Raymond and his fellow workers built a sawmill there and taught the local people to run it for profit. The children of both Christian and pagan were welcomed into the mission school. "In thirty years," wrote one missionary, "we shall see those who make the laws and who will constitute the very bone and sinew of the several nations to which they belong, no other than these poor ignorant boys and girls which we now have in our schools." And so, in many instances, it turned out.

Americans like Brother Raymond got on well with the people, and were sometimes even invited to arbitrate important and potentially murderous disputes between villages. On more than one occasion the British expressed alarm at the fervor of the Fourth-of-July celebrations in the neighborhood of Mo Tappan. On the other hand, the Americans lost out on a good many potential converts because they could not temper their rigid disapproval of drinking, smoking, and dancing—trespasses that most of the British missionaries were able to overlook.

For thirty years after Cinque's original defection, discouraging reports of him kept coming back to the mission. People said that he had become a trader, then a bandit, then a dealer in slaves. None of the rumors was true. For a long time it was believed that he had gone to the West Indies and had died there. But one day in 1879, an old, emaciated

African stumbled into the compound at the mission. No one was there who recognized him, but he said that he was Cinque and that he was dying. About a week later he breathed his last, and was buried among the graves of the American missionaries whose presence in Africa he had brought about. A sermon at his grave was preached by an American Negro missionary who had been born a slave.

The American Missionary Association, the outgrowth of the *Amistad* committee, continues to maintain missions in many parts of the world. The one in Sierra Leone was turned over to the United Brethren in Christ in the 1880s, a time when the freed slaves in the South pre-empted the Association's chief effort. The Negro colleges of Hampton, Talladega, LeMoyne, Dillard, Tougaloo, Huston-Tillotson, Atlanta, Fisk, and Howard were all established under the auspices of the Association. They still flourish, and are proud to trace their origins to the schooner *Amistad* and its brave black crew.

AFTERWORD

In 1843, not long after putting a temporary stop to Spanish complaints in the *Amistad* affair, Daniel Webster had some most surprising things to say about a case in which American slaves aboard a ship called the *Creole*, bound from Virginia to New Orleans, had mutinied and reached Nassau, where the British had set them free. Said Webster, "The British Government cannot but see that this case is one calling loudly for redress. . . . What duty or power, according to the principles of national intercourse, had they to inquire at all [into the status of the slaves]? . . . Surely the influence of local law cannot affect the relations of nations in any such matter as this." Señor Argaiz himself could hardly have put the argument better.

The reason for Webster's apparent change of point of view was his abiding distrust of England. He was opposed to slavery, but when it came to politics he was thoroughly sophisticated; and like many Americans, feared British intentions in the Caribbean.

In January 1843 Webster wrote to our consul in Havana to warn of a British plot to invade Cuba:

> Their agents are said to be now there, in great numbers, offering independence to the Creoles, on condition that they will unite with the colored people in effecting a general emancipation of the slaves, and in converting the Government into a *black Military Republic* under British protection. The British Abolitionists reckon on the naval force of their Government stationed at Jamaica, and elsewhere; and are said to have offered two large steam ships of war, and to have proposed to the Venezuelan General, Marino, who resides at Kingston, Jamaica, to take the command of an invading army. . . . If this scheme should succeed, the influence of Britain in this quarter, it is remarked, will be unlimited. With 600,000 blacks in Cuba and 800,000 in her West India islands, she will, it is said, strike a death blow at the existence of slavery in the United States. Intrenched at Havana and San Antonio, ports as impregnable as the rock of Gibraltar, she will be able to close the two entrances to the Gulf of Mexico, and even to prevent the free passage of the commerce of the United States over the Bahama banks, and through the Florida channel.
>
> The local authorities are believed not to be entirely ignorant of the perils which environ them, but are regarded as so torpid as not to be competent to understand the extent and imminency of those perils, nor the policy by which Great Britain is guided.

Webster adds that Great Britain must surely realize that any such action must bring on a major war and that therefore his source, though "highly respectable," may be unreliable. However, "many causes of excitement and alarm exist," and the United States must not disregard them.

AFTERWORD

John Calhoun succeeded Daniel Webster as Secretary of State in 1844, and from that time until the Lincoln administration, every Secretary of State and every President believed that the Supreme Court had made the wrong decision in the *Amistad* matter and that the Spanish government ought to be given indemnification. Every President mentioned the matter in a State of the Union speech. In 1844, at President Tyler's behest, the Committee on Foreign Affairs reviewed the whole case, and the committee chairman, Senator C. J. Ingersoll, of Pennsylvania, submitted a report recommending indemnity payments in the amount of seventy thousand dollars. Ingersoll's report put the year of the mutiny as 1840 instead of 1839—and used this date as evidence that the Africans had been in Cuba at least a year. He said that the evidence of "ignorant, half-civilized negroes" (meaning James Covey) and of a "self-styled African language expert" (Professor Gibbs) should not have been allowed. In further support of the committee's decision, Ingersoll included a letter written in 1818 by the then Spanish minister to Washington to our Secretary of State, a sort of white paper on the slavery situation in the Spanish colonies. The minister had written that because of "the total inaptitude of the Indians . . . the result of their ignorance of all the conveniences of life," it had been necessary to import Negro slaves.

> By the introduction of this system, the negroes, far from suffering additional evils, or being subjected, while in a state of slavery, to a more painful life than when possessed of freedom in their own country, obtained the inestimable advantage of a knowledge of the true God, and of all the benefits attendant on civilization.

The benevolent feelings of the sovereigns of Spain did

[153

not, however, at any time, permit their subjects to carry on this trade but by special licenses.

In 1818 Spain had agreed to outlaw the slave trade, because

> His Majesty discovered that the numbers of the native and free negroes had prodigiously increased under the mild regimen of the government and the humane treatment of the Spanish slave owners; that the white population had also greatly increased; that the climate is not so noxious to them as it was before the lands were cleared; and finally that the advantages resulting to the inhabitants of Africa in being transported to cultivated countries, are no longer so decided and exclusive, since England and the United States have engaged in the noble undertaking of civilizing them in their native country.

Senator Ingersoll added to this letter a diatribe against England for her antislavery policy. Robert Madden, the antislavery watchdog in Havana, was, he said, a "mercenary man, whose salary depended on his abolishing the slavery of Spanish negroes. His testimony, by itself, is wholly incredible." Ingersoll went on to imply that Madden was a political agent, paid to use the *Amistad* matter to stir up trouble between the United States and Spain, as well as between North and South. He concludes with an argument often heard in the 1840s and '50s: that American slaves are "better housed, fed, clothed and taken care of than the peasantry and poorer classes of most other countries, whose bondage is much more painful."

A bill supporting the committee's views passed the Senate but not the House. John Quincy Adams, now seventy-seven years old, vigorously opposed it and he had plenty of support, for North and South were beginning to vote sectionally on all slavery questions. A member from Ohio suggested that

AFTERWORD

indemnities should be paid instead to the Africans for the time they had spent in confinement and as recompense for having been deprived of their ship, the *Amistad*.

In 1846 James Buchanan, as Secretary of State under President Polk, recommended paying the Spanish claims, if only to be rid of the matter. An amendment, without a count of votes, was added to another bill, specifying a payment of fifty thousand dollars to Spain. But again, the House intervened. Mr. Adams, pale and in declining health, made it the subject of his only speech of the session. Such a payment would be, he said, "a robbery of the people of the United States. . . . Congress must decide if the Supreme Court decision is to be discarded."

So it went for the next fourteen years. Mr. Adams died in 1848, following a stroke suffered in the House, but his work in the *Amistad* matter had been well done and the Supreme Court decision was never tampered with. The report of the Committee on Foreign Affairs reappeared five times in the *Congressional Record*, the last time in 1858. The wrong date (1840 instead of 1839) was corrected on its third appearance. Our ministers to Spain found the subject a continual source of pain and annoyance; they were unable to complain about anything to the Spanish government without receiving an elegantly phrased equivalent of "Yes, but what about the *Amistad*?" After Washington Irving, who served in Madrid from 1842 to 1845, all the American ministers were from the South or of Southern sympathies and found the *Amistad* case particularly hard to bear.

Angel Calderón de la Barca, Spanish minister to Washington when the *Amistad* matter first came up, was reassigned there following a long tour of duty in Mexico City, and renewed his carping letters with gusto. He must have enjoyed a hearty, sardonic laugh when, in 1854, in response to one of

[155

his sorties, he received a letter from the American minister to Madrid, Pierre Soulé, a rabid slavery man who evidently did not know the history of the *Amistad* case. Said Soulé, "Your Excellency will not venture to intimate that there remains a doubt concerning the issue of that affair," and went on to predict imminent satisfaction for Spain.

Soulé made the mistake of agitating openly in Madrid for the American purchase of Cuba. The Spanish had never offered Cuba for sale and feared the word "purchase" was a euphemism. They asked for Soulé's removal. His successor was one Augustus Caesar Dodge, a friend of President Buchanan who had recently lost a senatorial race in Iowa. He spoke no French or Spanish and—possibly for this reason—did no harm in Madrid. The British minister said of him "though primitive to a degree in manners and social intercourse, he appears to me a very excellent person and one totally without guile." In 1858 Dodge wrote to Secretary of State Lewis Cass, "Vain though it be and is, I cannot refrain from the expression of my deep regret that Congress did not appropriate the funds. . . ."

Carl Schurz was our minister in 1860, appointed by Lincoln. Even he suggested that it might be well to get rid of the *Amistad* affair and that an indemnity payment could be concealed among other monies due to Spain. But Secretary of State Seward refused to consider it.

After the Civil War broke out and the American slaves were freed, Spain apparently decided that this particular cause was lost. The name *Amistad* was no longer mentioned either in official diplomatic correspondence or in Congress.

In 1883 the Milan Conference for Reform and Codification of the Law of Nations resolved to outlaw the extradition of slaves except in cases where a free man would be equally

AFTERWORD

subject to extradition. Spain promptly approved of this resolution. When a copy of it reached the Colonial Office in Madrid, someone added to it the notation that it was "in no way an innovation in Spain, whose ancient laws have always recognized as free the slave who enters the territory (including her own) of a nation where slavery does not exist, or who seeks refuge on board a ship belonging to such a nation."

APPENDIX I

From *A History of the Amistad Captives*

by John W. Barber (1840).

Map of part of Western Africa.

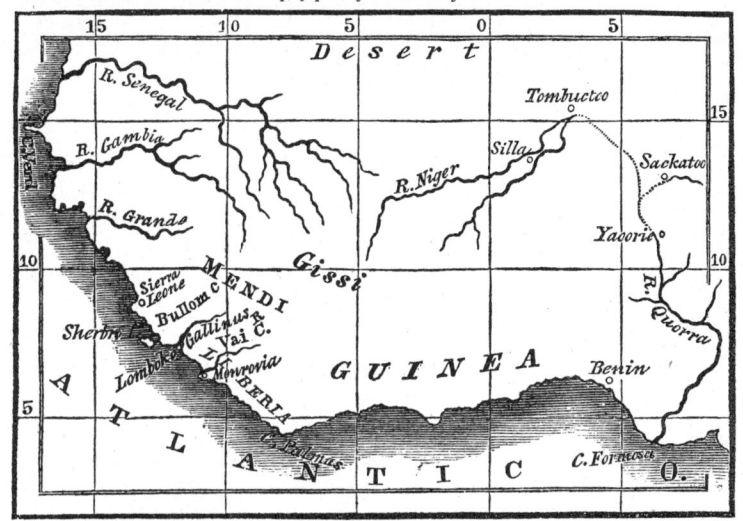

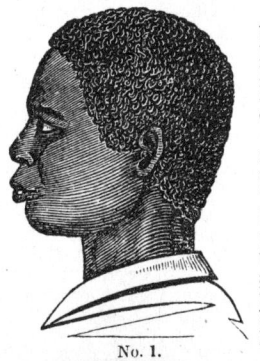

(1.) SING-GBE, [**Cin-gue,**] (generally spelt *Cinquez*) was born in Ma-ni, in Dzho-poa, *i. e.* in *the open land*, in the Men-di country. The distance from Mani to Lomboko, he says, is ten suns, or days. His mother is dead, and he lived with his father. He has a wife and three children, one son and two daughters. His son's name is *Ge-waw*, (God.) His king, Ka-lum-bo, lived at Kaw-men-di, a large town in the Mendi country. He is a planter of rice, and never owned or sold slaves. He was seized by four men, when traveling in the road, and his right hand tied to his neck. Ma-ya-gi-la-lo sold him to Ba-ma-dzha, son of Shaka, king of Gen-du-ma, in the Vai country. Bamadzha carried him to Lomboko and sold him to a Spaniard. He was with Mayagilalo three nights; with Bamadzha one month, and at Lomboko two months. He had heard of Pedro Blanco, who lived at Te-i-lu, near Lomboko.*

No. 1.

(2.) GI-LA-BA-RU, [**Grab-eau,**] (*have mercy on me*,) was born at Fu-lu, in the Mendi country, two moons' journey into the interior. His name in the public prints is generally spelt GRABEAU. He was the next after Cingue in command of the Amistad. His parents are dead, one brother and one sister living. He is married, but no children; he is a planter of rice. His king Baw-baw, lived at Fu-lu. He saw Cingue at Fulu and Fadzhinna, in Bombali. He was caught on the road when going to Taurang, in the Bandi country, to buy clothes. His uncle had bought two slaves in Bandi, and gave them in payment for a debt; one of them ran away, and he (Grabeau) was taken for him. He was sold to a Vai-man, who sold him to Laigo, a Spaniard, at Lomboko. Slaves in this place are put into a prison, two

No. 2.

---

* The following is a phrenological description of the head of Cingue as given by Mr. Fletcher: "Cingue appears to be about 26 years of age, of powerful frame, bilious and sanguine temperament, bilious predominating. His head by measurement is 22 3-8 inches in circumference, 15 inches from the root of the nose to the occipital protuberance over the top of the head, 15 inches from the Meatus Auditorious to do. over the head, and 5 3-4 inches through the head at destructiveness.

The development of the faculties is as follows: Firmness; self-esteem; hope—very large. Benevolence; veneration; conscientiousness; approbativeness; wonder; concentrativeness; inhabitiveness; comparison; form—large. Amativeness; philoprogenitiveness; adhesiveness; combativeness; de-are chained together by the legs, and the Spaniards give them rice and fish to eat. In his country has seen people write—they wrote from right to left. They have cows, sheep, and goats, and wear cotton cloth. Smoking tobacco is a common practice. None but the rich eat salt, it costs so much. Has seen leopards and elephants, the latter of which, are hunted for ivory. Grabeau is four feet eleven inches in height; very active, especially in turning somersets. Besides Mendi, he speaks Vai, Kon-no and Gissi. He aided John Ferry by his knowledge of Gissi, in the examination at Hartford.

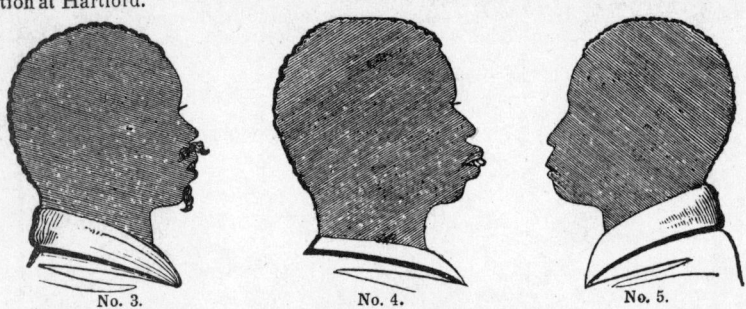

No. 3. No. 4. No. 5.

(3.) **Kimbo** (*cricket*) is 5 ft. 6 in. in height, with mustaches and long beard; in middle life, and is intelligent. He was born at Maw-ko-ba, a town in the Mendi country; his father was a gentleman, and after his death, his king took him for his slave, and gave him to his son Ban-ga, residing in the Bullom country. He was sold to a Bullom man, who sold him to a Spaniard at Lomboko. He counts thus: 1, etá ; 2, filí ; 3, kiau-wá ; 4, náeni ; 5, lóelu ; 6, wêta ; 7, wafurá ; 8, wayapá ; 9, tá-u ; 10, pu.— Never saw any books in his country. When people die in his country, they suppose the spirit lives, but where, they cannot tell.

(4.) NAZHA-U-LU, (*a water stick,*) also called from his country, **Kon-no-ma,** is 5 ft. 4 in. in height, has large lips, and projecting mouth, his incisor teeth pressed outward and filed, giving him rather a savage appearance; he is the one who was supposed to be a cannibal, (see page 5,) tattooed in the forehead with a diamond shaped figure. He was born in the Konno country: his language is not readily understood by Covey, the interpreter. Kon-no-ma recognizes many words in Mungo Park's Mandingo vocabulary.

(5.) **Bur-na,** the younger, height 5 ft. 2 in. lived in a small town in the Mendi country. He counts in Tim-ma-ni and Bullom. He was a blacksmith in his native village, and made hoes, axes, and knives; he also planted rice. He was sold for crim. con. to a Spaniard at Lomboko. He was taken in the road, and was four days in traveling to Lomboko. Has a wife and one child, a father, three sisters and brother living.

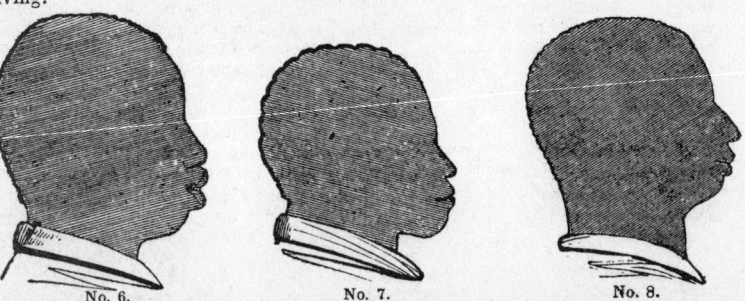

No. 6. No. 7. No. 8.

(6.) GBA-TU, [**Bar-tu,**] (*a club or sword,*) height 5 ft. 6 in. with a tattooed breast was born in the country of Tu-ma, near a large body of fresh water, called Ma-wu-a. His father is a gentleman and does no work. His king, named *Da-be,* resided in the

structiveness; secretiveness; constructiveness; caution; language; individuality; eventuality; causality; order—average. Alimentiveness; acquisitiveness; ideality; mirthfulness; imitation; size; weight; color; locality; number; time; tune—moderate and small. The head is well formed and such as a phrenologist admires. The coronal region being the largest, the frontal and occipital nearly balanced, and the basilar moderate. In fact, such an African head is seldom to be seen, and doubtless in other circumstances would have been an honor to his race."

town of Tu-ma. He was sent by his father to a village to buy clothes; on his return, he was seized by six men, and his hands tied behind; was ten days in going to Lomboko. There are high mountains in his country, rice is cultivated, people have guns; has seen elephants. *Remark.*—There is a village called Tu-ma, in the Timmani country, 60 miles from Sierra Leone, visited by Major Laing.

(7.) **Gna-kwoi** (in *Ba-lu* dialect, *second born*) was born at *Kong-go-la-hung*, the largest town in the Balu country. This town is situated on a large river called in Balu, *Za-li-ba;* and in Mendi, *Kal-wa-ra:* fish are caught in this river as large as a man's body—they are caught in nets and sometimes shot with guns. When going to the gold country to buy clothes, he was taken and sold to a Vai-man who sold him to a Spaniard named *Peli.* Gna-kwoi has a wife and one child; he calls himself a Balu-man; has learned the Mendi language since he was a slave; 5 ft. 6 in. in height.

(8.) **Kwong** was born at Mam-bui, a town in the Mendi country. When a boy he was called Ka-gnwaw-ni. Kwong is a Bullom name. He was sold by a Timmani gentleman in the Du-bu country, for crim. con. with his wife, to Luisi, a Spaniard, at Lomboko. He is in middle life, 5 ft. 6 in. high.

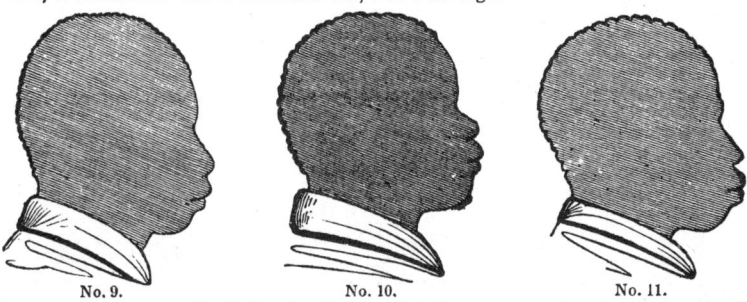

No. 9.   No. 10.   No. 11.

(9.) **Fu-li-wa,** Fu-li, (*sun,*) called by his fellow prisoners Fuliwa, (*great Fuli,*) to distinguish him from Fu-li-wu-lu, (*little Fuli,*) was born at Ma-no, a town in the Mendi country, where his king, *Ti-kba,* resided. He lived with his parents, and has five brothers. His town was surrounded by soldiers, some were killed, and he with the rest were taken prisoners. He passed through the Vai country, when taken to Lomboko, and was one month on the journey. He is in middle life, 5 ft. 3 in. high, face broad in the middle, with a slight beard. It was this Fuli who instituted the suit against Ruiz and Montez.

(10.) **P-ie,** *Pi-e,* or *Bi-a,* (5 ft. 4½ in. high,) calls himself a Timmani, and the father of Fu-li-wu-lu. He appears to have been distinguished for hunting in his country: says he has killed 5 leopards, 3 on the land, and 2 in the water; has killed three elephants. He has a very pleasant countenance; his hands are whitened by wounds received from the bursting of a gun barrel, which he had overloaded when showing his dexterity. He had a leopard's skin hung up on his hut, to show that he was a hunter. He has a wife and four children. He recognizes with great readiness the Timmani words and phrases contained in Winterbottom's account of Sierra Leone. He and his son seemed overjoyed to find an American who could articulate the sound of their native tongue.

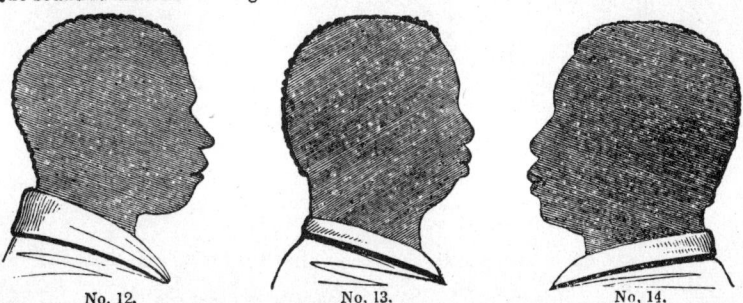

No. 12.   No. 13.   No. 14.

(11.) Pu-gnwaw-ni, [**Pung-wu-ni,**] (*a duck,*) 5 ft. 1 in. high, body tattooed, teeth filed, was born at Fe-baw, in Sando, between Mendi and Konno. His mother's brother sold him for a coat. He was taken in the night, and was taken a six days' journey, and sold to Garlobá, who had four wives. He staid with this man two years, and was employed in cultivating rice. His master's wives and children were employed in the same manner, and no distinction made in regard to labor.

(12.) **Ses-si,** 5 ft. 7½ in. with a sly and mirthful countenance, was born in Massa-kum, in the Bandi country, where his king, *Pa-ma-sa,* resided. He has three brothers, two sisters, a wife, and three children. He is a blacksmith, having learnt that trade of his brother; he made axes, hoes, and knives from iron obtained in the Mendi country. He was taken captive by soldiers and wounded in the leg. He was sold twice before he arrived at Lomboko, where he was kept about a month. Although a Bandi, he appears to have been able to talk in Mendi.

(13) **Mo-ru,** middle age, 5 ft. 8½ in. with full negro features, was born at Sanka, in the Bandi country. His parents died when he was a child. His master, Margoná, who sold him, had ten wives and many houses; he was twenty days on his journey to Lomboko. He was sold to Be-le-wa, (*great whiskers,*) i. e. to a Spaniard.

(14.) **Ndam-ma,** (*put on, or up,*) 5 ft. 3 in. a stout built youth, born in the Mendi country, on the river Ma-le. His father is dead, and he lived with his mother; has a brother and sister. He was taken in the road by twenty men, and was many days in traveling to Lomboko.

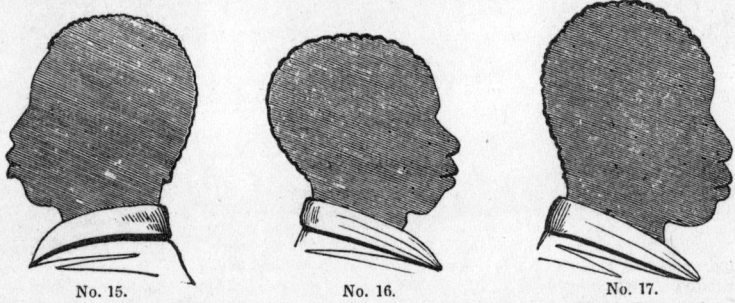

No. 15.   No. 16.   No. 17.

(15.) **Fu-li-wu-lu,** (*Fuli,*) or, as the name has been written, Furie, (*sun,*) called Fuliwulu, to distinguish him from Fuliwa, (*great Fuli,*) lived with his parents in the Timmani, near the Mendi country. He is the son of Pie, (No. 10.) He was taken with his father, by an African, who sold him to a Bullom man, who sold him to Luis, a Spaniard at Lomboko. He has a depression in the skull from a wound in the forehead. 5 ft. 2½ in. in height.

(16.) **Ba-u,** (*broke,*) 5 ft. 5 in. high, sober, intelligent looking, and rather slightly built. Has a wife and three children. He was caught in the bush by 4 men as he was going to plant rice; his left hand was tied to his neck; was ten days in going to Lomboko. He lived near a large river named Wo-wa. In his country all have to pay for their wives; for his, he had to pay 10 clothes, 1 goat, 1 gun, and plenty of mats; his mother made the cloth for him.

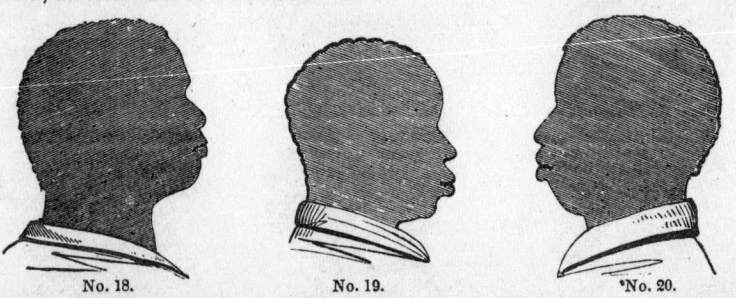

No. 18.   No. 19.   'No. 20.

(17.) **Ba,** (*have none,*) 5 ft. 4½ in. with a narrow and high head; in middle life. Parents living, 4 brothers and 4 sisters; has got a wife and child. He is a planter of rice. He was seized by two men in the road, and was sold to a Gallina Vai-man, who sold him to a Spaniard. High mountains in his country, but small streams; cotton cloth is manufactured, and hens, sheep, goats, cows, and wild hogs, are common.

(18.) **Shu-le**, (*water fall*,) 5 ft. 4 in. the oldest of the Amistad captives, and the fourth in command, when on board the schooner. He was born at Konabu, in the open land, in the Mendi country. He was taken for a slave by Ma-ya, for crim. con. with his wife. Momawru caught both him and his master Ma-ya, and made them slaves, and sold them to a man who sold him to the Spaniards at Lomboko. There is a large river in his country named *Wu-wa*, which runs from Gissi, passes through Mendi, and runs south into the Konno country.

(19.) **Ka-le**, (*bone*,) 5 ft. 4 in. small head and large under lip, young and pleasant. His parents living; has two sisters. He was taken while going to a town to buy rice. He was two months in traveling to Lomboko.

(20.) **Ba-gna**, (*sand* or *gravel*,) 5 ft. 3 in. was born at Du-gau-na, in the Konno country, where his king, *Da-ga*, lived. His parents are dead, and he lived with his brother, a planter of rice.

No. 21.   No. 22.   No. 23.

(21.) **Sa**, 5 ft. 2 in. a youth with a long narrow head. He was the only child of his parents, and was stolen when walking in the road, by two men. He was two months in traveling to Lomboko.

(22.) **Kin-na**, (*man* or *big man*,) 5 ft. 5½ in. has a bright countenance, is young, and, since he has been in New Haven, has been a good scholar. His parents and grandparents were living; has four brothers and one sister. He was born at Si-ma-bu, in the Mendi country; his king, Sa-mang, resided at the same place. He was seized when going to Kon-gol-li, by a Bullom man, who sold him to Luiz, at Lomboko.

(23.) NDZHA-GNWAW-NI, [**Nga-ho-ni**,] (*water bird*,) 5 ft. 9 in. with a large head, high cheek bones, in middle life. He has a wife and one child; he gave twenty clothes and one shawl for his wife. He lived in a mountainous country; his town was formerly fenced around, but now broken down. He was seized by four men when in a rice field, and was two weeks in traveling to Lomboko.

No. 24.   No. 25.   No. 26.

(24.) FANG, [**Fa-kin-na**,] 5 ft. 4 in. head elevated in the middle, stout built, and middle aged. He was born at Dzho-po-a-hu, in the Mendi country, at which place his father, *Baw-nge*, is chief or king. He has a wife and two children; was caught in the bushes by a Mendi man, belonging to a party with guns, and says he was ten days in traveling to Lomboko after being a slave to the man that took him, less than a month.

(25.) FAHI-DZHIN-NA, [**Fa-gin-na**,] (*twin*,) 5 ft. 4 in. marked on the face with the small pox; was born at Tom-bo-lu, a town of Bombali, in the Mendi country. He was made a slave by Tamu for crim. con. with his wife. Tamu sold him to a

Mendi man, who sold him to Laigo, a Spaniard, the same who purchased Grabeau. He says many people in his country have the small pox, to cure which, they oil their bodies.

(26.) **Ya-boi,** 5 ft. 7 in. large head, stout built, and in middle life; was born at Kon-do-wa-lu, where his king, Ka-kbe-ni, (*lazy,*) resided. His village was surrounded by soldiers, and he was taken by Gillewa, a Mendi man, to whom he was a slave ten years. Had a wife and one child. Gillewa sold him to Luiz, the Spaniard.

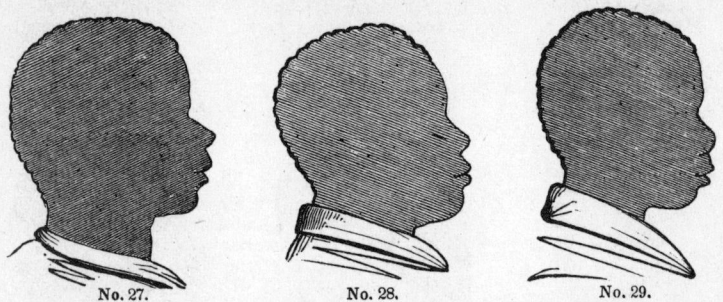

No. 27.   No. 28.   No. 29.

(27.) **Fa-ban-na,** (*remember,*) 5 ft. 5 in. large round head, tattooed on the breast; in middle life; he and Grabeau were from the same country, both having the same king. He has two wives and one child; all lived in one house. His village was surrounded by soldiers: he was taken prisoner, sold twice, the last time to a Spaniard at Lomboko.

(28.) **Tsu-ka-ma,** (*a learner,*) 5 ft. 5½ in. young, with a pleasant countenance; was born at Sun-ga-ru, in the Mendi country, where his king, Gnam-be, resided: has parents living, 3 sisters, and 4 brothers. He was taken and sold into the Bullom country, where he lived for a time with his master, who sold him to Luiz, at Lomboko.

(29.) BE-RI, [**Ber-ri,**] (*stick,*) 5 ft. 3 in. with mustaches and beard, broad nose; in middle life. He was born at *Fang-te,* in Gula, a large fenced town, where his king, Ge-le-wa, resided. He was taken by soldiers, and was sold to Shaka, king of Genduma, in the Vai or Gallina country, who sold him to a Spaniard. Genduma is on a fresh water river, called *Boba.* It is three or four miles from the river, and nine from the sea.

No. 30.   No. 31.   No. 32.

(30.) FAW-NI, [**Fo-ni,**] 5 ft. 2 in. stout built; in middle life. He was born at Bum-be, a large town in the Mendi country: the name of his king was Ka-ban-du. He is married, and has parents, brothers, and sisters living. He was seized by two men as he was going to plant rice. He was carried to Bem-be-law, in the Vai country, and sold to Luiz, who kept him there two months, before he took him to Lomboko. From Bem-be-law to Lomboko is one day's walk.

(31.) **Bur-na,** (*twin,*) the elder, has a cast in the eye; was taken when going to the next town, by three men. His father is dead, and he lived with his mother; has four sisters and two brothers. When his father died his brother married; all lived in the same house. In his country are high mountains, but no rivers; has seen elephants and leopards. He was six weeks in traveling to Lomboko, where he was kept three and a half moons.

(32.) **Shuma,** (*falling water,*) 5 ft. 6 in. with mustaches and beard; in middle life. He can count in the Mendi, Timmani, and Bullom. His parents have been dead a long time; has a wife and one child, was taken prisoner in war, and it was four moons after he was taken, before he arrived at Lomboko. Shuma spoke over the corpse of Tua, after the Rev. Mr. Bacon's prayer. The substance of what he said, as translated by Covey, was, "Now Tua dead, God takes Tua,—we are left behind—No one can die but once," &c.

No. 33.   No. 34.   No. 35.

(33.) **Ka-li,** (*bone,*) 4 ft. 3 in. a small boy, with a large head, flat and broad nose, stout built. He says his parents are living; has a sister and brother; was stolen when in the street, and was about a month in traveling to Lomboko.

(34.) **Te-me,** (*frog,*) 4 ft. 3 in. a young girl, says she lived with her mother, with an elder brother, and sister; her father was dead. A party of men in the night broke into her mother's house, and made them prisoners; she never saw her mother or brother afterwards, and was a long time in traveling to Lomboko.

(35.) **Ka-gne,** (*country,*) 4 ft. 3 in. a young girl. She counts in Mendi like Kwong, she also counts in Fai or Gallina, imperfectly. She says her parents are living, and has four brothers and four sisters; she was put in pawn for a debt by her father which not being paid, she was sold into slavery, and was many days in going to Lomboko.

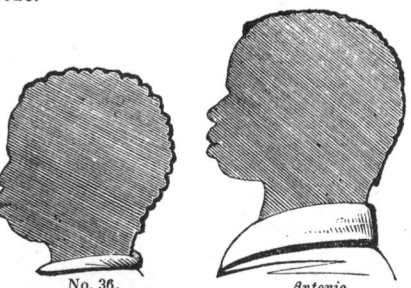

(36.) **Mar-gru,** (*black snake,*) 4 ft. 3 in. a young girl, with a large, high forehead; her parents were living; she had four sisters and two brothers; she was pawned by her father for a debt, which being unpaid, she was sold into slavery.

The foregoing list comprises all the Africans captured with the Amistad, now [May, 1840] living. Six have died while they have been in New Haven; viz. 1, *Fa,* Sept. 3d, 1839; 2, *Tua* (a Bullom name) died Sept. 11th; 3, *We-lu-wa* (a Bandi name) died Sept. 14th; 4, *Ka-ba,* a Mendi man, died Dec. 31st; 5, *Ka-pe-li,* a Mendi youth, died Oct. 30; 6, *Yam-mo-ni,* in middle life, died Nov. 4th.

No. 36.   Antonio.

JAMES COVEY, the interpreter for the Africans, is apparently about 20 years of age; was born at Benderi, in the Mendi country. His father was of Kon-no descent, and his mother Gissi. Covey was taken by three men, in the evening, from his parents' house, at Go-la-hung, whither they had removed when he was quite young. He was carried to the Bullom country, and sold as a slave to Ba-yi-mi, who resided at Mani. He lived there for three years, and was employed to plant rice for the wife of Ba-yi-mi, who treated him with great kindness. He was sold to a Portuguese, living near Mani, who carried him, with 200 or 300 others to Lomboko, for the purpose of being transported to America. After staying in this place about one month, Covey was put on board a Portuguese slave-ship, which, after being out about four days from Lomboko, was captured by a British armed vessel, and carried into Sierra Leone. Covey thus obtained his freedom, and remained in this place five or six years, and was taught to read and write the English language, in the schools of the Church Missionary Society. Covey's original name was *Kaw-we-li,* which signifies, in Mendi, *war road,* i. e., a road dangerous to pass, for fear of being taken captive. His Christian name, James, was given him by Rev. J. W. Weeks, a Church Missionary, at Sierra Leone. In Nov., 1838, he enlisted as a sailor on board the British brig of war Buzzard, commanded by Captain Fitzgerald. It was on board this vessel, when at New York, in Oct., 1839, that James was found, amid some twenty native Africans, and by the kindness of captain Fitzgerald, his services as an interpreter were procured.

James Covey.

APPENDIX II

The *Antelope* Case

In the spring of 1820, in violation of a law forbidding American citizens to engage in the slave trade, the American captain of a Baltimore-built privateer, the *Columbia,* changed his ship's colors to those of one of the newly revolted Spanish colonies of South America, "La Plata" (subsequently Venezuela) and her name to the *Arraganta*. He then set her course for the coast of Africa, with the hope of capturing a Spanish slaver or two. On the way, she took aboard twenty-five slaves from an American privateer out of Bristol, Rhode Island, and a hundred and fifty-six from a ship sailing under Portuguese colors. She then overtook and captured a Spanish slaver called the *Antelope,* which had just left a West African slave depot and had more than two hundred slaves aboard. With this prize in tow, the *Arraganta* sailed for Brazil, where the captain intended to sell all the slaves. But near the Brazilian coast, the *Arraganta* was wrecked. Her captain was drowned, but most of the others aboard survived and managed to reach the *Antelope*. The *Arraganta's* mate, a Mr. Smith, took over as captain, ran up the colors of La Plata,

APPENDIX II

and gave the *Antelope* a new name, *General Ramirez*. He then made for the Southern coast of the United States with the object of disposing of the slaves illegally.

Off Florida the slave ship was captured by the *Dallas*, a brig of the United States Coast Guard, in command of a Captain Jackson, and brought into Savannah. Captain Smith boldly demanded restitution of the ship and cargo in behalf of the Republic of La Plata. This claim was dismissed with costs by both District and Circuit Courts. Smith and his American crew were, in fact, in violation of two laws: they were engaging in the slave trade and they were participating in a Spanish colonial war against the strictly neutral policy of our government.

But the dismissal of Smith's claim was only the beginning of the case of the *Antelope*. Captain Jackson, of the *Dallas*, filed a libel for forfeiture under the law forbidding Americans to engage in slaving. The Spanish government filed a claim for the *Antelope* and the Africans who were on board her when the Americans took the ship; and the Portuguese government filed for those Africans taken by the *Arraganta* from the Portuguese ship. The Spanish cited the Treaty of 1795, with emphasis on Article 8 and its phrase about "rescue from pirates." On the other hand, the United States District Attorney argued that all the slaves should go free and be transported back to Africa, in accordance with the antislave-trade Act of Congress of 1818. Lawyers for the *Dallas* captain argued that only those Africans who had been on the ship from Rhode Island should go free, and that Captain Jackson should have twenty-five dollars a head for each one of them, besides complete title to the *Antelope* and all the remaining Africans.

It was seven months before the district judge gave his verdict, which was that Captain Jackson was entitled to one-fourth the value of all the surviving slaves; that the slaves from the Rhode Island ship should go free, and that the others should be handed over to the Spanish and Portuguese governments. By this time, forty-four of the slaves who had landed at Savannah had died and there was no way of knowing which had come from which ship. In Savannah there were neither abolitionists nor theological students to try to communicate with them. Nobody attempted to ask them anything, or even considered doing so. Remanded to the custody of the United States Marshal, who charged the government sixteen cents a head per day for their board and keep, they had been put to work building fortifications.

The decision satisfied nobody. The District Attorney thought Captain Jackson's portion was too low, while the Spanish government thought it too high. Both appealed to the Circuit Court. The Portuguese now dropped out of the picture, because no Portuguese owners had come forward to press claims and there was some doubt as to whether the slaver had, in fact, been Portuguese, or had merely been sailing under Portuguese colors. Spain, at that date, had outlawed slaving north of the equator, and Spanish ships often found it convenient, when in North Atlantic waters, to keep a Portuguese flag on hand.

The court clerk at Savannah reported that all but seven of the slaves from the Rhode Island ship were now dead. But this seemed an oddly high percentage compared to mortality among those who were not to be freed. In May 1821 the Circuit Court judge arbitrarily raised the number of surviving slaves from the Rhode Island ship from seven to sixteen. He canceled the delivery of any slaves to Portugal and reduced Captain Jackson's per capita salvage claim, adding that he doubted whether there should be a salvage claim at all, and if there were one, whether it should not go to the government of La Plata. Since there was no sure way of choosing the sixteen to be liberated—the word of the slaves themselves would not have been legally admissible, even had they understood what was going on—the judge decreed a lottery.

APPENDIX II

The *Antelope,* along with those slaves originally on board her, should be returned to Spain. The other slaves must await further rulings.

The District Attorney, even more dissatisfied than before, appealed to the Supreme Court. And, in due course—five years after the capture of the *Antelope*—Chief Justice John Marshall read the verdict. The salvage ruling was confirmed. The slaves from the Rhode Island ship were to be freed and so were those from the allegedly Portuguese ship. The *Antelope* and her slaves were to be returned to Spain, but the Spanish owners must offer proof of ownership. There was to be no lottery. "Having been sanctioned by the usage and consent of almost all civilized nations," the slave trade could not be called internationally illegal, "however unjust and unnatural" it might be. But the owners must prove their claim. This, of course, was very difficult, but there was a Spanish officer of the *Antelope* who volunteered to swear that he knew and recognized thirty-nine of the Africans. These thirty-nine were handed over to the Spanish Vice-Consul at Savannah, while the others were returned to the coast of Africa in an American naval vessel. Besides those who had died, one was missing, and one, according to an enigmatic note in the court records, "discharged."

In rendering the verdict, Chief Justice Marshall emphasized that the case was not to be regarded as a precedent. But in 1839, in connection with the *Amistad* case, Attorney General Grundy offered it as one, declaring that the affair of the *Antelope* had certainly established the precedent that American law could not affect Spanish law; and "that a foreign vessel engaged in the African slave trade, captured on the high seas in time of peace by an American cruiser, and brought in for adjudication, would be restored." Furthermore, in the *Antelope* case, the Africans had never even been within the territorial limits of Spanish territory, whereas in the case of the *Amistad* they most certainly had. The *Amistad,* in fact, was not officially a slave trader, but merely a

APPENDIX II

cargo ship taking property from one part of Cuba to another. Grundy wrote, "I consider the facts as stated, so far as this Government is concerned, as establishing a right of ownership to the negroes in question."

The *Antelope* case did not end with the Supreme Court decision. Two more years of litigation followed, concerning who was to pay the costs, which came to more than thirty-six thousand dollars—an enormous sum for those days. The Circuit Court ruled that the Portuguese, having got nothing, should pay nothing, while the Spanish should pay a proportion in ratio to the value of the thirty-nine slaves returned to them. The United States Marshal's sixteen-cents-a-day bill now added up to three hundred and fifty dollars a head. In the end, it was the United States government that paid for everything.

BIBLIOGRAPHY

The chief sources used in preparing this book were the New Haven, New London, Hartford, New York, and Washington newspapers of the day; the official court records; the *Congressional Record;* the diaries of John Quincy Adams; and the archives of the American Missionary Association.

In addition, the following books were found useful:

Abel, A. H., and Klingberg, F. J. (eds.). The Tappan Papers, Library of Congress Mss. Collection.

Abel, A. H., and Klingberg, F. J. *A Side-light of Anglo-American Relations, 1839–59.* Lancaster, Pa., 1927.

Baldwin, Roger S. *Argument before the Supreme Court in the case of the United States, appellants, vs. Cinque and others, Africans of the Amistad.* New York, 1841.

Baldwin, Simeon. Paper read to the New Haven Historical Society, May 17, 1886.

Barber, John W. *A History of the Amistad Captives.* New York, 1840.

Bartlett, Ellen Strong. "The Amistad Captives." *New England Magazine.* March 1900.

BIBLIOGRAPHY

Bemis, Samuel Flagg. *John Quincy Adams and the Union.* New York, 1949.

Birney, William. *James G. Birney and His Times.* New York, 1890.

Bohannan, Paul. *Africa and Africans.* New York, 1964.

Bowers, Claude. *The Spanish Adventures of Washington Irving.* Boston, 1940.

Bushnell, Horace. *A Discourse on the Slavery Question.* Hartford, 1839.

Crosby, K. H. "Polygamy in the Mende Country." *Africa.* July 1857.

Curtin, Philip D. *The Image of Africa.* Madison, Wisc., 1964.

Davidson, Basil. *Black Mother.* Boston, 1961.

Dinsmore, Charles Allen. "Voyage of the Amistad." *Yale University Library Gazette.* January 1935.

Duberman, Martin B. *Charles Francis Adams.* Boston, 1960.

Duckett, Alvin Laroy. *John Forsyth.* Athens, Ga., 1962.

Ettinger, Amos A. *The Soule Mission to Spain.* New Haven, 1932.

Fenton, J. S. *Outline of Native Law in Sierra Leone.* Freetown, 1948.

Fyfe, Christopher. *A History of Sierra Leone.* New York, 1962.

Goddard, T. N. *A Handbook of Sierra Leone.* London, 1925.

Goodrich, Samuel Griswold. *A History of Africa.* Louisville, 1850.

Guenebault, J. H. *A Natural History of the Negro Race.* London, 1837.

Herskovits, Melville Jean. *The Human Factor in Changing Africa.* New York, 1961.

———. *The Myth of the Negro Past.* New York, 1941.

Hollander, Barnett. *Slavery in America.* New York, 1963.

Jarrett, H. R. *A Geography of West Africa.* London, 1956.

Kimble, George (ed.). *Tropical Africa.* New York, 1960.

Kup, A. Peter. *A History of Sierra Leone, 1400–1787.* New York, 1961.

Little, K. L. *The Mende of Sierra Leone.* London, 1951.

Macy, Jesse. *The Anti-Slavery Crusade.* New Haven, 1919.

Madden, R. R. *A Letter to William Ellery Channing Regarding the Slavetrade in Cuba.* Boston, 1839.

McClendon, R. Earl. "The Amistad Claims." *Political Science Quarterly*. September 1933.

Migeod, Frederick William Hugh. *A View of Sierra Leone*. London, 1926.

Morse, John T. *John Quincy Adams*. Boston, 1883.

McKitrick, Eric L. (ed.). *Slavery Defended*. New York, 1963.

Odell, George C. D. *Annals of the New York Stage*. New York, 1928.

Prichard, James Cowles. *The Natural History of Man*. London, 1842.

Pelzer, Louis. *Augustus Caesar Dodge*. Iowa City, Iowa, 1908.

Pierson, H. W. *American Missionary Memorial*. New York, 1853.

Rankin, F. Harrison. *A Visit to Sierra Leone in 1834*. Philadelphia, 1835.

Schlesinger, Arthur M. *The Age of Jackson*. Boston, 1945.

Seward, William H. *Life and Public Services of John Quincy Adams*. New York, 1855.

Smith, Edwin W. (ed.). *African Ideas of God*. London, 1950.

Sturge, Joseph. *A Visit to the United States in 1841*. London, 1842.

Tappan, Lewis. *The Life of Arthur Tappan*. New York, 1870.

Thompson, George. *Thompson in Africa*. Cleveland, 1852.

Walker, S. A. *Church Missions in Sierra Leone*. London, 1847.

Welch, Galbraith. *Africa before They Came*. New York, 1965.

Winterbottom, Thomas. *An Account of the Native Africans in the Neighbourhood of Sierra Leone*. London, 1803.

INDEX

Abolitionists, 12, 19-23, 26, 39, 41, 56, 60-61, 63-66, 79, 91, 114-115, 131
Adams, Charles Francis, 80
Adams, John Quincy, 18-19, 109, 131, 154-55; argues Amistads' case, 87-108; supports Amistads, 64-66, 76-85
Africa, 4, 6, 38-39, 40-41, 46, 49, 61, 71, 75, 107, 109; climate, 134-37; culture, 110-14; missionaries in, 119, 123, 125-32, 138-50
American Bible Society, 21, 22
American Board of Missions, 126
American Colonization Society, 19, 21-22, 126
American Education Society, 21
American Missionary Association, 147, 150
American Missionary Society, 119
American revolution, 89
American Sunday School Union, 21
American Tract Society, 21
Amistads, *passim;* abolitionists and, 19-23, 109-10, 114-18; Adams argues for, 87-106; captured, 7; culture, 110-14; defense of, 26-27, 86, 87-99; hearings for, 12-16, 40-43; language, 33-34, 69-70, 83; life masks, 161-67; missionaries and, 125-32, 135-50; morale, 122-23; return to Africa, 134-35; Supreme Court decision on, 107-108; tell their story, 51-55; on tour, 119-22, 128-29; treatment of, 28-30, 47-50; trial, 69-75
Anglo-Spanish antislavery treaty, 26-27, 35, 60, 45-46, 60, 97
Antelope case, 45, 102, 105, 169-173
Antislavery; *see* Abolitionists
Antislavery Depository, 76
Antislavery Society, 21
Anti-slave-trade law of 1808, 107-108, 170
Antonio, 7, 14-15, 28, 37, 72-73, 75, 115
Argaiz, Pedro Alcántara, 44-45, 46-47, 57-58, 68, 92, 93-94, 98, 101, 115-17, 151
Arraganta, 169
Artists Fund Society, 122

[179

INDEX

Bacon, Francis, 73
Bacon, Leonard, 33
Bahamas, 8
Baldwin, Henry, 84
Baldwin, Roger, 26, 40-41, 42, 69, 73, 74, 78-80, 86, 88, 107, 108, 109
Ban-na, 130
Barber, John W., 159
Barbour, Philip P., 84, 100
Bar-ma, 73, 122
Barnegat Bay, 4
Bible, 50-51, 121, 131
Birney, James, 131
Black Schooner, The, or the Pirate Slaver, 37-38
Blanco, Pedro, 51-52, 73-74, 127
Blossom, 3
Booth, Mr., 118, 123, 127-28
Boston, 5, 16, 45
Bowery Theatre, 37-38
Brazil, 169
British Antislavery Commission, 59, 61, 63, 91
Broadway Tabernacle, 131
Buchanan, James, 155, 156
Bur-na, 36, 49, 51
Buzzard, 51
"By a Calm Observer," 60

Calderón de la Barca, Angel, 23-26, 35, 44, 89-93, 97, 155-56
Calhoun, John, 77, 88, 153
Caribbean, 52, 63, 151
Cass, Lewis, 156
Catron, John, 84
Causten, John, 85
Channing, William Ellery, 60
Christianity, 110-11, 132, 135, 145
Cinque ("Joseph Cinquez"), 12-13, 17, 28-31, 37, 39, 47, 48, 52, 53-55, 70-73, 75, 80, 110, 113-14, 118, 119-23, 128, 130-32, 134, 139-40, 142, 143, 149-50
Cinque Park, 130
Civil War, 156
Clay, Henry, 22
Coast Guard, U.S., 6, 16, 107, 170
Colonizationism, 33, 84

Combe, George, 31
Committee for the Defense of the Africans of the *Armistad*, 23, 127, 128, 147
Congressional Record, 155
Connecticut, 38, 43, 59, 75, 92, 110
Constitutional liberties, 89-91
Courant (Hartford), 37
Courier & Enquirer (New York), 56
Court decisions, 17, 42-43, 75, 78, 107
Courts, protection of, 94-95, 97
Covey, James, 51, 69-71, 129, 147, 153
Crandall, Prudence, 11-12, 22
Creole, 151
Cuba, 25, 27, 35, 41, 56, 57, 60-64, 74, 90-91, 95, 100, 152
Currier & Ives, 77

Daily Express (New York), 27, 36, 39
Daily Herald (New Haven), 8-9, 13, 39, 47, 70, 71, 129
Dallas, 170
Day, George E., 33, 71-72
Decatur, Stephen, 83
Declaration of Independence, 81, 89, 97, 104-105
Dodge, Augustus Caesar, 156
Dred Scott decision, 84

Elements of International Law, 101
Ellsworth, William, 26, 74
Emancipados, 62
Emancipator, 22, 63, 122
Emerson, Ralph Waldo, 65, 87
Emmeline, 4-5
England, 3, 26, 52, 86; antislavery treaty with Spain, 35, 60, 97; Cromwellian, 114; missionaries from, 135-38, 141-42, 148-49; territorial ambitions, 63-64, 151-152

Fa, 145
Fa-ban-na, 145
Farmington, 36, 117, 122-23, 127, 129

180]

INDEX

Ferrer, Ramón, 7-8
Ferry, John, 34, 47, 51
Fletcher, Mr., 30-32
Fon-ne, 55, 123, 130
Fordham, Peletiah, 5-6
Forsyth, John, 23, 24, 26, 34-35, 44, 46, 57-59, 68, 76, 82, 89-90, 92-95, 97, 98, 101, 116
Fox, Henry S., 64, 97
Franklin, Benjamin, 21
Freetown, 33, 34, 51, 52, 127, 134-140, 142, 146
Fu-li, 118-19
Fulton, 5

Gag Rule, 65, 81
Gallaudet, Dr., 47
Garrison, William Lloyd, 22
Gazette (New London), 9, 16, 32, 39
Gedney, Lieutenant, 7, 8, 11, 14, 19, 35, 42, 68-71, 74, 75, 83, 88-89, 102, 107
General Union for Promoting the Observance of the Christian Sabbath, 21
Gentleman, 129, 131-32, 134, 147
George III, 89
Gerry, Elbridge, 81
Gibbs, Josiah Willard, 33-34, 51, 69-70, 72, 153
Gibbs, William, 33n.
Gil-a-ba-ru, 50
Gilpin, Henry, 82, 86, 106
Globe (New York), 3, 4
Grabeau, 70, 72, 75, 80, 123
Grampus, 67-68, 76, 103
Green, Henry, 5-6, 41, 43, 69, 74, 75
Grundy, Felix, 45-46, 82, 101-102, 172-73
Gubernativamente, 94
Guenebault, J. H., 111, 112

Harndon, Ann, 142-43, 144
Harrison, William Henry, 82
Hartford, 36, 40
Havana, 7, 15, 27, 52, 54, 59, 61-64, 68, 115, 154

Henry VIII, 88
"High seas" defined, 59
History of the Armistad Captives, A, 159-67
Holabird, William S., 10-12, 19, 26, 34-35, 40, 41, 46, 68-69, 73-74, 76, 95
Hooker, Dr. Charles, 48

Indemnification, 116, 153, 155, 156
Indians, 4, 153
Ingersoll, C. J., 153
International law, 77-78, 101-102, 116
Irving, Washington, 155
Isabella II, Queen, 58
Isham, General, 70, 73, 75
Islam, 137-38

Jackson, Andrew, 20, 23, 62, 63, 84
Jackson, Captain, 170-71
Jay, John, 22, 122
Jay, William, 18, 22, 65
Jefferson, Thomas, 62, 78
Jocelyn, Nathaniel, 30, 37, 122
Jocelyn, Simeon, 22, 131, 140-41
Judson, Andrew T., 11-12, 16, 26, 34, 43, 47, 59, 63, 71, 75, 76, 83, 107

Ka-le, 83, 109, 120, 143, 144
Ka-pe-ri, 50
Ke-ne, 114-15, 143
Kidnapped, 114
Kidnapping, 27, 52, 55, 107
Kim-bo, 50, 55
Kin-na, 53, 83, 110, 118, 121, 123, 131, 138-39, 145, 147
Knights of Malta, 41
Ko-no-ma, 32, 48
Kreo (dialect), 51

Ladinos, 77
Law, African and European compared, 112-13
Leary, Jerome, 85
Leavitt, Joshua, 22, 28-29, 48, 132
Lexington, 77
Liberator, 22

[181]

INDEX

Liberia, 19, 84, 119
Lincoln, Abraham, 153, 156
Lo-ko-ma, 143
Lomboko, 51-52, 73-74
Long Island, 5-6, 74
Loring, Ellis Gray, 79

McKinley, John, 84
McLean, John, 84
Madden, Dr. Robert, 59-64, 70, 100, 154
Malaria, 137-38
Malta, 41
Mandingo, 29n.
Mar-gru ("Sarah"), 114-15, 131, 143, 144-46, 148
Marshall, John, 172
Massachusetts, 12, 66
Meade, Lieutenant, 8, 14, 15, 36, 42, 74, 102
Mende (language), 33-34, 36, 51, 54, 70
Mendeland, 78, 83; climate, 137; customs, 110-14, 134-35; missionaries to, 119, 123, 134-50; war in, 127, 139; weaving in, 121
Merchandise, slaves as, 89-90, 95, 103, 107, 115
Milan Conference for Reform and Codification of the Law of Nations, 156
Missionaries, 4, 110, 118-21, 125-132, 135-50
Mission schools, 148-49
Mobs, 20-21
Montes, Pedro, 7-8, 10, 11, 12, 15-16, 27, 35, 36, 39, 41, 46, 54, 55-58, 72-74, 93, 95, 98, 107, 115, 116-17
Mo Tappan, 147, 149
Moultrop, Mr., 30
Mutiny, 14-16, 19, 27, 90

Nashua & Andover Railroad, 121
Navy, U.S., 5, 67
Negro colleges, 150
New Haven, 17, 22, 28, 110, 129
New London, 8, 9, 12, 17, 23

New York, 5, 12, 20-21, 37-38, 43, 59, 93, 98
New York Magdalen Society, 21
New York Manumission Society, 22
Niger Expedition, 137-38

Oberlin College, 22, 128
Official Journal of the Executive Administration, 104

Paine, Lieutenant, 68, 103
Pendleton, Colonel, 28, 29, 72, 79, 114
Pennsylvania Abolitionist Society, 21
Philology, 33
Phrenology, 31
Piracy, 24, 42, 45, 59, 107
Polk administration, 63, 155
Polygamy, 111, 137, 139
Porter, Dr. Noah, 129
Portugal, 52, 61, 169-71, 173
Postal laws, 20
Presidential power, 91-92, 97-98, 103, 117
Protest movements, 19
Puerto Príncipe, 7, 14, 53, 64
Puerto Rico, 25, 91

Randolph, John, 86
Randolph, Virginia, 62
Raymond, Eliza, 138
Raymond, William, 126-28, 132, 135, 139-46
"Regarding the Slave Trade in Cuba," 60
Register (New Haven), 57, 114
Ruiz, José, 7-8, 11, 12, 14-16, 27, 35, 36, 37, 39, 41, 46, 52, 54, 55-58, 64, 72-74, 83, 93, 95, 98, 101, 102, 107, 115, 116-17

Salvage rights, 11, 16, 23, 35, 43, 72, 74, 75, 107, 171-72
Schurz, Carl, 156
Secret societies, 110, 134-35
Sedgwick, Theodore, 26, 35, 36, 69, 74, 79
Senate resolutions, 77-78, 81, 88

INDEX

Seward, William, 156
Sierra Leone, 34, 54, 73, 119, 127, 133, 134-37
Slave insurrections, 25
Slavery, 42; apologia for, 104; attitudes toward, in 1839, 19; in Cuba, 60-64, 74, 90, 100; extradition, 156-57; illegal under Spanish law, 26-27, 35, 75, 102; tribal, 52, 114; *see also* Abolitionists, Slave traders
Slave ships, 52, 61, 169-73
Slave traders, 38, 51-52, 60-62, 71, 73-74, 75, 95, 97, 114, 127
S-ma, 130
Smith, Captain, 169-70
"Society and Civilization," 81
Society for the Extinction of the Slave Trade and the Civilization of Africa, 137
Soulé, Pierre, 156
South Carolina, 19-20
Spain, 3, 23, 40, 41, 57-58, 60, 63, 157; *Antelope* case and, 170-73; antislavery laws, 26-27, 35, 45, 74, 75, 86, 90, 97, 102; indemnification due, 153-54, 156; Treaty of 1795 with, 24-25, 95-96
Staples, Seth, 26, 35, 40, 69, 74, 79
Star (Long Island), 39
Steele, James, 128, 135, 139-41
Stevenson, Robert Louis, 114
Story, Joseph, 84, 107
Sturge, Joseph, 119, 129
Supreme Court, 3, 85-86, 155; accepts Amistads' case, 78-80; decision, 107; hearing, 87-106

Taney, Roger B., 84, 85, 100
Tappan, Arthur, 20-22
Tappan, Benjamin, 21
Tappan, John, 21
Tappan, Lewis, 21, 29, 36, 42, 63, 79, 109, 110, 114, 118, 119, 124, 125-27, 128-32, 138, 139-140, 145, 146
Teçora, 52

Te-me, 114-15, 143
Temne (tribe), 127
Texas, 61, 63-64
Thirty Years' War, 112
Thompson, George, 146-48
Thompson, Smith, 40, 42-43, 77, 78, 84
Tombs (prison), 56
Townsend, Amos, 110, 114
Treaty of Ghent, 97
Treaty of Guadelupe-Hidalgo, 63
Treaty of 1795, 24-25, 35, 41, 46, 59, 75, 94, 95-96, 102, 107, 117, 170
Trist, Nicholas P., 61-63, 78
Trumbull, John, 81
Trumbull, Mr., 72
Tu-a, 50
Tucker, Chief, 142, 145-46, 148
Turkey, 41
Tyler, John, 82, 116, 129, 153

Union Missionary Society, 21
United Brethren in Christ, 150

Van Buren, Martin, 4, 11, 35, 36, 46, 64, 68, 75, 76
Victoria, Queen, 31, 64

War, tribal, 127, 139
War of 1812, 84
Washington, 6-7, 8, 10-12, 14, 23, 43, 69, 73-74
Wayne, James Moore, 84
Webster, Daniel, 21, 115-16, 151-152, 153
West Indies, 49, 86, 149
Westville, 79, 80, 109, 114
Whigs, 80
Wilcox, Norris, 43, 71, 72, 80
Williams, A. F., 118, 122-23, 130
Wilson, Henry, 128, 135, 140, 148
Wilson, Tamar, 128, 140, 147

Yale Divinity School, 33, 47, 76, 79, 148

[183

FOR THE BEST IN PAPERBACKS, LOOK FOR THE 🐧

In every corner of the world, on every subject under the sun, Penguin represents quality and variety—the very best in publishing today.

For complete information about books available from Penguin—including Puffins, Penguin Classics, and Arkana—and how to order them, write to us at the appropriate address below. Please note that for copyright reasons the selection of books varies from country to country.

In the United Kingdom: Please write to *Dept. JC, Penguin Books Ltd, FREEPOST, West Drayton, Middlesex UB7 0BR.*

If you have any difficulty in obtaining a title, please send your order with the correct money, plus ten percent for postage and packaging, to *P.O. Box No. 11, West Drayton, Middlesex UB7 0BR*

In the United States: Please write to *Consumer Sales, Penguin USA, P.O. Box 999, Dept. 17109, Bergenfield, New Jersey 07621-0120.* VISA and MasterCard holders call 1-800-253-6476 to order all Penguin titles

In Canada: Please write to *Penguin Books Canada Ltd, 10 Alcorn Avenue, Suite 300, Toronto, Ontario M4V 3B2*

In Australia: Please write to *Penguin Books Australia Ltd, P.O. Box 257, Ringwood, Victoria 3134*

In New Zealand: Please write to *Penguin Books (NZ) Ltd, Private Bag 102902, North Shore Mail Centre, Auckland 10*

In India: Please write to *Penguin Books India Pvt Ltd, 706 Eros Apartments, 56 Nehru Place, New Delhi 110 019*

In the Netherlands: Please write to *Penguin Books Netherlands bv, Postbus 3507, NL-1001 AH Amsterdam*

In Germany: Please write to *Penguin Books Deutschland GmbH, Metzlerstrasse 26, 60594 Frankfurt am Main*

In Spain: Please write to *Penguin Books S. A., Bravo Murillo 19, 1° B, 28015 Madrid*

In Italy: Please write to *Penguin Italia s.r.l., Via Felice Casati 20, I-20124 Milano*

In France: Please write to *Penguin France S. A., 17 rue Lejeune, F-31000 Toulouse*

In Japan: Please write to *Penguin Books Japan, Ishikiribashi Building, 2-5-4, Suido, Bunkyo-ku, Tokyo 112*

In Greece: Please write to *Penguin Hellas Ltd, Dimocritou 3, GR-106 71 Athens*

In South Africa: Please write to *Longman Penguin Southern Africa (Pty) Ltd, Private Bag X08, Bertsham 2013*